DISCOVERING GOD'S PRESENCE

Robert F. Morneau

THE LITURGICAL PRESS

Collegeville   Minnesota

Acknowledgement: Chapters 1–3, 7, 11–13, and 15 originally appeared as articles in *Sisters Today,* with the following titles: "Aboutness: Religious Life Once-Removed" (November 1973); "Towering: Sharing a Faith Perspective" (June–July 1977); "The Healing Power of Poetry" (March 1979); "The ERRA Principle of Prayer" (May 1976); "The Ho-Ho, Hum-Hum Principle" (December 1974); "Prepositional Christianity" (January 1978); "The Ministry of Surprise" (April 1979); "Beyond Death and Dying" (April 1978).

Chapter 4 appeared in *Contemplative Review,* with the title "The Divine Host and Hesitant Guest: A Commentary on George Herbert's Poem 'Love'" (Winter 1977).

Chapter 5 appeared in *Spiritual Life,* with the title "Psalm 100: A Mini-Theology" (Spring 1977).

Chapters 6, 8–10, and 14 appeared in *Review for Religious,* with the following titles: "Principles of Prayer" (May 1979); "Integration and the Sacrament of Reconciliation" (January 1978); "Spiritual Staying Power: Homeostasis" (September 1978); "St. Augustine: Insights and Challenges" (September 1977); "Chapter Delegate: Qualities and Responsibilities" (May 1977).

Published with permission.

Library of Congress Cataloging in Publication Data

Morneau, Robert F   1938–
   Discovering God's presence.

   1. Spiritual life—Catholic authors—Addresses, essays, lectures.   I. Title.
BX2350.2.M683   230'.2   80-18590
ISBN 0-8146-1197-4

Nihil obstat: Joseph C. Kremer, S.T.L., *Censor deputatus. Imprimatur:* ✚George H. Speltz, Bishop of St. Cloud, Minnesota, June 4, 1980.
Printed in the United States of America.
Photos by Herb Montgomery. Cover design by Placid Stuckenschneider, O.S.B.

DEDICATION

to the
Students and Faculty,
Administration and Staff
of
Silver Lake College
Manitowoc, Wisconsin
1966–1978

Contents

DISCOVERING GOD'S PRESENCE

Introduction

A fundamental truth underlying all experience is the presence of God. Faith, that precious gem beyond price, allows that truth to inform our consciousness and to direct our hearts. An active faith situates us in a divine milieu wherein we view people as our brothers and sisters, we see God as our Father, Brother and Spirit, we reverence creation as an entrustment, we sense our own dignity and preciousness, we relate all events to the mystery of Love, the core of reality. Faith is powerful and active; through it we learn to love life in its foundation and principle. Caryll Houselander once wrote:

> The Being of God, then, presses upon man. It is his environment. It sings to him in the winds. When he touches grass or water, he touches it with his fingers; he smells it in fields of hay and clover and in newly cut wood; he listens to it in the falling of the rain and the murmur of the sea. He tastes it in the food that he eats; he sees it in the flowers beneath his feet; he is clothed in it in silk and wool. Its measured beat in his own blood rocks him to sleep with the coming darkness and wakens him with the light. He receives it in the sunlight like a sacrament that gives life (*The Reed of God*, New York: Sheed & Ward, 1973, 80–81).

The practice of the presence of God has many expressions, as many as our own countenances in the face of different experiences. One expression is that of clarity and conciseness: herein we come to know what the nature and essence of God's presence is. Another expression is a frown: we search in apparent helplessness for a hidden Lord. With inquisitive eyes we trace the cause of his presence and what the effects might be. Though simple in nature, this presence of God is complex in our experience.

Over the past eight years, I have written a number of articles, each of which I thought was distinct from the other, lacking any single principle of unity. Upon further reflection, however, I have come to realize that, though the angle varied at times and the subject matter seemed to be diverse, all the articles were rooted in a single truth: God's presence. Each time we revisit this Reality we come away enriched, knowing more about ourselves and our Creator. The Mona Lisa retains its enigma despite countless viewings; much more does the mystery of our God deepen upon each showing. The following portraits are mere hints and clues of an incomprehensible God who shares his life, his presence, with us and who, wonder of wonders, longs that we share our lives, our presence, with him.

Preview

Presence and Perplexity——Aboutness: Religious Life Once-Removed. A sound distinction that is worthy of reflection is the difference between knowing about God and knowing God himself. The former is a spectator approach demanding little risk and no commitment; the latter is a personal relationship transforming one's very life. "Aboutness" connotes an unwillingness or an inability to enter into life fully and freely. This can happen in any walk of life and, though the article applies "aboutness" to religious life, it can be transposed to any vocation. God's presence demands "directness"; it is not experienced in "aboutness."

Presence and Perspective——Towering: Sharing a Faith Perspective. People journey to mountain peaks to scan in one breathtaking moment a vast horizon. Moses made the journey as did the prophets of all ages and creeds. Vision demands height. What we see often depends on what we are. Faith vision gives us a view of what our God is like and who we are, made to his image and likeness. Perspective fosters seeing; seeing implies being truly present to the Presence.

Presence and Poetry——Healing Power in Poetry. The poet is a gifted seer! The poem reveals an invisible kingdom reserved for the sensitive and the silent. Faith poetry, concerned with the Good and Beautiful and True, opens to us new horizons of God's presence and workings. Our thirsting and bruised spirits are healed and enriched as the poet sings of the glory of God.

Presence and Praise——Divine Host and Hesitant Guest in George Herbert's Poem "Love." The Christian God is a God of revelation. Dialogue with his creatures is a way of life. We are constantly invited to enter into his presence and to partake of his love. With good cause, we hesitate to come before the living and true God, awestruck by his glory and sensitive to our own unworthiness. George Herbert records his confrontation with the presence of the Lord, and we come quickly to realize that his story is indeed our story.

Presence and a Psalm——Psalm 100: A Mini-Theology. The Hebrew songs of the Old Testament speak powerfully of God's working in history. The psalmist, gifted with insight and words, shares his experience of God's presence. By reflecting attentively on the psalm we can be drawn back into the original experience, i.e., the stirrings and movements of God in our lives. By storing psalms in the memory of our hearts, we have an effective means of practicing the presence of God in the paths of our daily lives.

Presence and Principles——Principles of Prayer. The patterns of the seasons, the movements of the stars, the structure of the invisible atom, all tell of an incredibly rich design and Designer. God's presence can be discerned in all his art works; in a special way, in the dialogue with his creature, the human person. By pondering the principles and patterns of prayer, we witness how God works in our life and what guidelines we might use to live more deeply before his face.

Presence and Prayer——The ERRA Principle of Prayer. Through the quietness of prayer we encounter in a special way the presence of God. This dialogic process fosters our relationship with God and with each other. Prayer is a multi-faceted reality: prayer of experience and encounter, prayer of reflection and meditation, prayer of response and affection, prayer of articulation and expression. God comes to us in many forms of prayer and it is well that we know the value and nature of each.

Presence and Peace——Integration and Reconciliation. A deep need within our lives is the need for peace. This comes as a gift in knowing that our relationships with God, others, self, and world are whole and integral. A channel for this wholeness comes through the Christian community in the sacrament of reconciliation. By means of word and sign we encounter Jesus as he extends to us the Father's forgiveness and peace. The mystery of sin, that attitude-act whereby we separate ourselves from God and his creation, is confronted in this sacrament. Reconciliation restores the presence that sin attempts to annihilate.

Presence and Power——Spiritual Staying Power. The wisdom and power of God permeate every moment of every day. By his wisdom we are gifted with insight and vision; by his power we are enabled to be a faithful people, fulfilling his plan of salvation through love and forgiveness. St. Paul derived stability and hidden strength because of the Christ who lived within him. All was related to this single Source; nothing could separate him from the love of Jesus. Thus, by a profound and simple principle ("to live through love in his presence") Paul's life had a constancy amid many turbulent moments.

Presence and Pedagogue——Augustine: Insights and Challenges. God's presence manifests itself throughout creation: the stars, the earth, events of history, time and space. Yet, given this universal presence, it is in the human person that the Lord comes to us in incredible ways. One of the great channels and instruments of God's presence is St. Augustine—scholar, sinner, singer, and saint. Gifted with words that flowed from the deep recesses of his mind and heart, God's dwelling place, Augustine shares with us some insights and challenges that draw us to appreciate and respond to our Father's call.

Presence and Potpourri——The Ho-Ho, Hum-Hum Principle. Though human experience is universal in its roots, each age presents new circumstances that demand appropriate responses. In an age characterized by depression, divorce, deceit, and deadly dignity, the Christian community witnesses to hope, hospitality, humility, and humor. These gracious dispositions give entry into the world of God's presence, a presence that is life-giving and pointed to the fullness of joy.

Presence and Prepositions——Prepositional Christianity. A sensitive esteem for prepositions can enrich our spiritual development. Entering into the heart of the *with* ("Know that I am with you always"), joining hands with the *for* ("This is my body given for you"), tasting the tears of the *in* ("We will make our home in you"): all speak of a profound style of presence. As God is a God who is with, for and in us, so too we are challenged to share that same type of presence with each other.

Presence and Play——Ministry of Surprise. The life we are called to give to one another as Christians is packaged in diverse ways. The delight of surprise and play manifests God's presence in a unique and joyful manner. We are caught off guard by a sunset, an unexpected letter, a voice from the forgotten past. Being surprised by our God, there comes a call to serve others by making our Father's presence felt in unexpected, playful ways.

Presence and Pragmatism——Qualities and Responsibilities of a Chapter Delegate. The deliberative process is central to our democratic process; it is also essential in any community life. The Church is community, and God often speaks to us through the discernment of the community. Though this article addresses itself to religious life and the deliberation of annual meetings (chapters), the qualities and responsibilities also apply to our family meetings, our parish council assemblies, our political gatherings. The qualities described make God present; the responsibilities fulfilled bring about the kingdom.

Presence and Possibility——Beyond Death and Dying. What lies beyond death? What type of presence, if any, can we anticipate when life on earth is concluded? The topic of death and dying has been extremely popular during this past decade. The Christian perspective presents possibilities that transcend the answers of secular humanism. Our Christian hope tells us that we are to expect the fullness of God's presence beyond the portals of death. Here we will participate fully in the mystery of presence which we now taste only in bits and pieces.

Proposal

I propose but a single reflection in these essays: that the more lovingly conscious we are of our Father's presence, the more meaningful, joyful and active our lives will be. To live this will be to share the experience of Teilhard de Chardin:

> God, in all that is most living and incarnate in him, is not far away from us, altogether apart from the world we see, touch, hear, smell and taste about us. Rather he awaits us every instant in our action, in the work of the moment. There is a sense in which he is at the tip of my pen, my spade, my brush, my needle—of my heart and of my thought (*The Divine Milieu*, New York: Harper & Row, 1957, 64).

1

Presence and Perplexity
Aboutness: Religious Life Once-Removed

Joseph Conrad, the Polish-born English novelist, wrote this personally provocative statement: "I remember I preferred the soldier to the philosopher at the time; a preference which life has only confirmed." Conrad's radical choice in approaching life and its various dimensions is a choice which confronts every individual. The decision to be a soldier, implying a strong activism and vital involvement, appeals to a world of speed, change and movement. The choice of philosophizing speaks more of passivity and quiet withdrawal, which offer to some a security and peace so welcomed by the human spirit. Perhaps the alternative choices of life could be expressed in this manner: is there a tendency in the present period of history toward living and experiencing, or do most people opt for self-introspection, detailed analyses, studied criticism, psychoanalysis, constant reflection?

Obviously we must avoid the common either-or fallacy. The human condition and lived situation is not either experience or reflection, either living or analyzing, either life or thought, either love or reason, either contemplation or meditation. Rather, the situation in which all of us find ourselves is one of both-and. In some way we must blend these various aspects of life into a meaningful whole. Our choices are as complex as our personhood. Although there is no inherent opposition in the tendencies mentioned above, yet there is always the perennial danger of myopia, narrowing our vision and ideal by focusing on one aspect of life to the exclusion of all others.

The consequences of such short-sightedness are an anxious emptiness and a continual disappointment in life itself. The question thus emerges with special urgency of whether in religious life there is a subtle but definite feeling and tendency toward one or the other pole. Has today's religious chosen a life of experience or of reflection? If, to any significant degree, an exclusive choice has been made, there will arise an unrest and discontent stronger than that of mere winter. This chapter has as its purpose to expose an extreme, the extreme of being caught up in "aboutness."

Much of life is consumed by poring over the experiences of others. Our reading, observing, studying do not offer direct experiences of the life situation under direct consideration. The overwhelming quantity of reading material, the ubiquitous television set, and even the multiplicity of personal relationships can fragment the minds and hearts of contemporary men and women. Toffler's *Future Shock* well documents this fact. Getting caught up in the plurality of activities, persons and things, one could almost slip into a spectator-type of lifestyle in which life itself is once-removed. Like a sports fan in the stands, one is always watching, sometimes cheering or booing, but never playing the game. A haunting, tragic feeling begins to emerge, subtle and vague at first but increasingly obvious, that "life-is-passing-one-by."

What compounds the situation is that when firsthand experiences do come along, a person might not even trust in this reality since, for such a person, reality is essentially reflective rather than lived. Such a life becomes one of "aboutness"—about Christianity, about death, about love, about hope, about grace. Words, always once-removed from experiences which they are articulating, become the core of life rather than the reality which they express. For the "about person" the primary direct experience might take the strange shape of frustration about the "aboutness"; this is quickly followed by the twin of frustration, fear. One becomes afraid of experiencing things deeply; Hopkins' "the dearest freshness deep down things" has no meaning for such a person. Frustration and fear block the possibility of making a total and complete commitment.

Presuming that experiencing deeply has become difficult for the contemporary person for the reasons stated, it would seem to follow that religious life has been affected by this unhappy malady. The religious, like all people exposed to contemporary culture, can become once-removed from life. One's energies and time can be absorbed by reflecting, reading, talking about commitment, about poverty, about obedience, about chastity. As for experiencing being poor, living in openness and responsiveness to the word of God, preserving an inner integrity and order through disciplined love, there simply is not time with so much to read about and to reflect on in these areas of religious life.

Such a facetious and hyperbolic statement is made for the sake of stressing a point. Not so humorous, however, is the fact that our times witness considerable unrest and confusion, so obvious in the vocation problem, the authority crisis, the painful exodus. Thus it would not be wise to leave uncovered any facet that might shed some light on possible solutions to such a dilemma. The existential sense of anxiety, the pervasive feeling of alienation and the growing sense of distance from being (life) elicit our grave and, it is to be hoped, our therapeutic concern.

To be cut off from fundamentals and basics, from essentials and rudiments, from experience and life itself, whether this severing is caused by thought, fear, drugs or any other form of slavery, results first of all in an almost undetectable sickness leading swiftly but surely to termination of all life functions, physical as well as spiritual. Any style or form of life removed from the immediacy of God, people and things will quickly lose its flavor and challenge. Self-consciousness and reflective analysis are posterior to the excitement of word and deed; we must not reverse the order of things. Standing back and judging are prerogatives of those who have been warriors of involvement and participation. The small child who sits on the dock while others are enjoying the water will never drown, but will not have real happiness and joy either. Life is risky. The gospel warns us of the consequences of keeping our lives wrapped up snugly in our security blankets.

On occasion, the "aboutness" feeling does vanish: in the rich moments of play, in the corridors of laughter and humor, in the silence of deep prayer, in the glance of love, in the sudden smile of a friend, in the ecstasy of song. It is as if one were embraced by reality in these "surprises of joy," a seemingly passive activity only to those devoid of experience. The bonding that swells forth at such times melts hostility, dispels fears, tears down defenses; an ontological oneness and a sense of belonging surface if only for the briefest moment, but a moment that permeates life with joy and hope, a moment that will feed the memory in less propitious times. For the graced individual who sheds the fog and nebulosity of "aboutness" and replaces it with direct experience, there will be a new wealth from which to draw meaningful reflections and meditations rich in insight. A strong tension manifesting itself in religious life is the approach to vows in terms of "aboutness": speaking about poverty yet having so much; struggling with theories about obedience yet retaining one's own will with tenacity; longing for an exclusive relationship with Christ and yet thinking about chastity-celibacy as though that vow were not necessary for such a relationship.

Poverty

A religious can reflect upon the meaning of poverty without acting in accord with the essence of it for just so long before one's sense of integrity and authenticity begins to break down. Thinking about poverty no doubt will produce a variety of valid if not profound insights: one can be materially poor, elderly poor, handicapped poor, emotionally poor, morally poor, spiritually poor. But then the moment of testing arrives. How has one's reflecting on the reality found expression in life, in repeated patterns of behavior? Does the truth of one's reflections, ranging from the quality dimension of poor (as an attitude of mind) to the quantity dimension (where having too much or too little dehumanizes), actually penetrate one's life in such a way that the value conceived and desired now emerges in daily life? Is one poor in fact or only in theory? Is there a personal experience leading to the radical conviction that one is poor and that all is basically gift? Many people today are seeking a level of honesty and authenticity which is admirable. But there are many obstacles infringing upon the attempts to live an honest poverty. An intellectually and materially affluent society does not foster such a value nor does a culture which is frequently obsessed with security and protection. Unless opportunities to live gospel poverty are offered or made, there will be a continued loss of credibility not only within the religious life but also for those not vowed to such ideals.

Although there are no simplistic answers to the poverty problem, the answer is not really difficult. Intellectually the distinctions between want and need, accidental and essential, useful and necessary are relatively easy; the problem lies in the doing. Several comments are in order: any type of poverty leading to ineffective service is false and a lie; development of security which removes all risk and eliminates trust in God's providence is pagan; living in luxury and superfluity cannot be justified. To avoid the type of religious life that is once-removed, the experience of not having time, money, energy, pleasure and even life itself for the sake of God and others must be present to some degree. Otherwise the vow made before God and the human community was simply a vow *about* poverty.

Obedience

Obedience and authority, those familiar but unpopular symbiotic twins, have fallen on hard times. The voice of personal freedom rings out loud and clear, though not always on pitch, even to the point of taking over the opera completely in arias so self-absorbing as to forget that there is anyone else in the cast! A cursory knowledge of history brings us back to reality: both obedience and freedom are necessary components of life and there is no intrinsic incompatibility between them. It is obvious to all that the extremes of authoritarianism (not yet dead but in intensive care) and individualism (extremely robust if not downright obese) have done their damage; enslavement to either means certain death.

But the question of the function of obedience in contemporary religious life still calls for an answer: does the religious today in fact experience the reality of obedience or has this dimension of religious life also wandered into the twilight zone of thinking *about* obedience? Do religious do what they want to do or what they feel they must do, regardless of who the authority figures happen to be? Is the level of obedience confined to one's relationship to the community and duly elected superiors, or does it also apply even more directly to God's personal commands and the needs of others, even those lying far beyond the precincts of community? At the heart of obedience two basically inseparable moments dwell: listening and responding. To whom one listens and the degree of generosity with which one responds specify the type and value of obedience under discussion. Certainly listening and responding predominantly to oneself, though perhaps at times necessary, fail to qualify as fulfilling the vow of obedience.

If the speaker is God and our response flows from hearing his word, no one can deny that the vow in its deepest recesses is being lived out. The major problem is that of discernment: the ability to discover God's plan in a given situation. This discerning type of obedience for most people lacks the necessary clarity, assurance and specification needed for communal life. Perhaps the ultimate causes underlying such a situation are distrust of oneself and constant danger of self-deception. Thus emerges the problem of directly experiencing obedience by listening to and responding to human authority, which might be described as incarnational obedience. Here it is that individual freedom and personal conscience confront an army of problems. Does authority really know me in asking that I assume these responsibilities? Does this type of regulation or directive foster personal and communal growth as well as respect human dignity? Is this request within the area of those possessing authority?

The extremes of a legalistic, total submission to whatever is asked and the demand for absolute certitude about the wisdom and fairness of every directive can be quickly disposed of as anachronistic. The issue centers upon giving up freedom in certain areas of life for the sake of others and obeying authoritative directives one hopes are arrived at through the mutual collaboration of all concerned. But if, as a matter of fact, one completely determines one's own future, what possible meaning does obedience have? In reality there would be no experience in reference to this vow. The religious, attempting to maintain at least verbal authenticity, would have to explain obedience in terms of personal freedom, a neat trick demanding ingenuity, well-developed mental if not logical gymnastics, and a slight touch of sophism. A return to the sixteenth-century "God-me" theology offers no possible solution to the obedience problem; yet how close is our century to the sixteenth! The divorce (or temporary legal separation) of freedom and obedience will be reconciled only when authority proves itself benevolent and person-centered in the best sense of those terms, and when individuals break from American pragmatic individualism and return to the deep social-community consciousness demanded by the gospel. On that day, the "about" obedience syndrome will yield to a freeing of self for full involvement in being for others.

Chastity

C. S. Lewis has written that the most unpopular virtue of Christianity is chastity. In a culture such as ours, so marvelous and challenging yet so destructive and materialistic, there have been and still are many distortions and illusions about human sexuality that confirm the statement of Lewis. Not only is chastity an unpopular virtue for many, but it is seen as an impossibility if not a dangerous and Manichean abnormality.

Perhaps the term celibacy rather than chastity expresses more clearly the reality behind this dimension of religious life. Negatively, celibacy has reference to abstention and detachment from a most beautiful area of human love. Marital love that ideally is both personal and relational has brought much happiness and holiness into the lives of many people. A keen and profound appreciation of this God-given human reality allows a person who knowingly and freely accepts celibacy to offer to God and the Church a great sacrifice and gift, one which is tremendously pleasing to God since it symbolizes life and love in itself.

On the positive side of this celibate consecration, a relationship is established with Christ and his people that is unique and exclusive, a relationship flowing from a special calling from God. In service and complete dedication one can be for others as Christ was and is. Married love, also the result of a special call, has a different form of service and total dedication. The important thing is the love: the expression is a truly significant dimension in the life of the Church and thus must be fostered and protected with great care and reverence. The question arises: is there a tendency today to speak about the vow rather than to experience it by total commitment to the person of Christ and the needs of his people? This experience will demand knowledge and sensitivity to the values involved in such a dedication. It will demand a generosity and spirit of sacrifice of no small account. It will demand God's help and the support of the community.

In describing mental illness we often say that the ill person is no longer in touch with reality. Any form of illness or lack of health, whether it be personal, interpersonal, social or spiritual, has the quality of being at least once-removed from directly experiencing reality. Religious life is not exempt from the fundamental rules for good health. It cannot afford the luxury of an "aboutness" existence, especially in the crucial areas of the vows.

Christ, the exemplar for every religious, was actually poor; his existence was one of obedience; his celibacy told of a singular expression of love. Probably the only totally "non-about" person in history was the Lord. Because Christ was a soldier in Conrad's sense, he was justified in being a philosopher. Thus we find in him both the expression of the good news and its realization.

2

Presence and Perspective
Towering: Sharing a Faith Perspective

A wildlife marsh in central Wisconsin was recently gifted with an observatory tower, making possible a total view of the marsh with its ever-changing life. Curious lovers of nature, eager to transcend the narrow, ground-level perspective of this region, climb the tower to see the vast workings of nature in one panoramic view. In this act of "towering," they gain new insights, discover diverse patterns of relationships, and come to a new appreciation of many particular facets of nature. Filled with excitement and an urge to share this new vision, the "towering" observers hurry down to narrate what they have seen and felt to anyone willing to listen. Then, though vicariously, the listener "towers" with the observers and shares their perspective.

Every writer, artist and story teller is simply sharing experiences seen from his or her personal observatory. What is seen (objective dimension), how it is viewed (subjective aspect), and the manner of its articulation (communicative process) are important. If there is successful perception, an accurate comprehension and effective use of signs and symbols, the miracle of dialogue results in a mutual vision and a profound communal experience. However, attempting to share experiences is difficult, especially on the faith level. The element of mystery, the limitations of language, and the variety of possible religious experiences foster subtle ambiguities. Yet, even though there may be only partial success, both the challenge of the adventure and the importance of growing in faith certainly make the endeavor well worth every effort.

Rembrandt captured in shades and colors the beauty of the country and the human form; Beethoven embraced in music profound inner experiences of majesty and glory; Shakespeare captured in words the joys and agonies of the human spirit. Faith experiences have also been shared in word and life: the Gospels, the lives of the saints, the writings of Augustine, John of the Cross, and thousands of others down through the ages. Though only those skilled in various techniques might be able to express in various forms their deep inner experiences, the fact remains that every Christian has a faith vision, however implicit. This vision varies according to education, life experiences and cultural influences. Yet a basic framework underlies the Christian life. This essay is one of possible hundreds of "towering visions" delineating that framework. Its accuracy and potential for integrating various aspects of the Christian life are limited by the incomprehensibility of the subject matter and by the finite capacities of the observer.

A faith vision centers on the reality of God and not on man/woman. Though tempted often by the forces of a myopic humanism, the human person must struggle to avoid positioning self at the center of the stage or at the hub of the wheel. Because this temptation succeeds in capturing the heart of the human, God, if he is fortunate, comes away with a supporting actor's award or a reluctant acknowledgment that he is a necessary spoke in the wheel of life. A tower vision of Christianity must be absolutely clear on priorities: God is central and all else is secondary to this *fact*. This God is active in his love, and he constantly speaks his word, doing the truth throughout history.

The person of faith, like a robin with cocked ear attentive to any subterranean movement of a spring worm, is first of all a *listener:* a listener to a speaking and loving God. If listening, and not just hearing, occurs, the faith person responds. It is presupposed that a discerning process is taking place to make sure (at least relatively sure) that one is listening to God and not to the many possible destructive forces stirring within the inner person. A faith-discerned response is the obedience manifested so clearly in the life of Jesus; he listened to the voice of his Father and lived the call. Consistent and meaningful responses are grounded in various dispositions (virtues). The cultivation of these through prayer and fasting is indispensable to growth in the Spirit. Finally, the basic process of this Christian vision of a God speaking-loving, of a person listening-responding by means of properly disposed powers, culminates in a sense of identity. Our self-image and eventual self-acceptance results at the end and not the beginning of this process.

From the observatory tower, five different but logically related perspectives will now be shared. Each of the five perspectives will follow the above framework, which is summarized in this diagram:

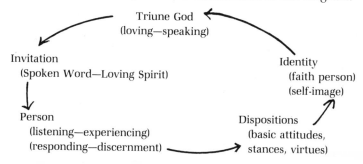

Perspective A: From Fidelity to Song

Both the Old and New Testaments are emphatic in relating that God is a God of fidelity. He has given his word; he has made a promise that is always being fulfilled. From Abraham to the prophets, from Jesus to the Pentecost event, the Father is always working and bringing his life to all creation. By contrast, John Courtney Murray's work, *The Problem of God,* opposes our infidelity to God's fidelity: "Over against the inconsistency and infidelity of the people, who continually absent themselves from God, the name Yahweh affirms the constancy of God, His unchangeable fidelity to His promise of presence." St. Paul speaks of this fidelity in terms of trust: "You can trust God not to let you be tried beyond your strength, and with any trial he will give you a way out of it and the strength to bear it" (1 Cor 10:13). The Book of Exodus adds other qualities besides fidelity to Yahweh:

> Yahweh passed before him and proclaimed, "Yahweh, Yahweh, a God of tenderness and compassion, slow to anger, rich in kindness and faithfulness; for thousands he maintains his kindness, forgives faults, transgression, sin. . . ." And Moses bowed down to the ground at once and worshipped (34:6-8).

God's fidelity breaks forth into the mystery and the invitation to intimacy. The infinite longing for oneness is clearly seen in Jesus' sacerdotal prayer in the Gospel of John. The goal of the kingdom is a total oneness: an intimate bonding of God and all creation. This invitation is filled with warmth and affection; it calls for a total commitment because it flows from a total love. Humankind is invited to make its home in God. Failure to respond ends in death. Indeed, "to walk out of his will is to walk nowhere" (C. S. Lewis). God's will is that through love we may experience his peace and joy. Everyone's vocation is radically the same: to rejoice in the intimacy of a faithful God, to strive for and be open to holiness. God's fidelity is dynamic; it draws us to himself.

The Response of Praise. If God is known in his fidelity, if this invitation to intimacy is sensed to any degree, the healthy and spontaneous response would be nothing less than joyous praise. This praise centers on the being and majesty of God himself. In the face of such goodness and tenderness, a profound song leaps forth from the heart of anyone graced to be in the presence of holiness. Praise is basically an affective acknowledgment of excellence; the religious person acknowledges warmly who God is and what he has done and continues to do throughout creation. Praise becomes a way of life for anyone in tune with the living and true God. Not to adore is to remain in darkness; it is to be outside of reality. Alfred Lord Tennyson's poem "Flower in the Crannied Wall" shows how such an apparently insignificant experience can lead to God, and we can sense the implicit praise between the lines:

> Flower in the crannied wall,
> I pluck you out of the crannies,
> I hold you here, root and all, in my hand,
> Little flower—but *if* I could understand
> What you are, root and all, and all in all,
> I should know what God and man is.

As we praise this God of fidelity who has called all creation into profound intimacy, we must examine how such praise is really possible. What underlying disposition makes feasible this new vision by us? The answers lie in a most precious gift that God offers to us, the gift of faith. Faith makes possible a close personal relationship with God. The results of this grace are the discovery of a new world, the vision which now sees all things differently, the formation of a new person. Lacking this gracious power, reality remains blurred, vague and essentially empty. To continue to survive, we clutter life with many distractions, but a persistent feeling of meaninglessness and a sense of going nowhere haunt the human spirit. Walter Kerr captured this sensation: "We can distract ourselves while we are publicly occupied;

the sense of going nowhere overtakes us precisely when we are going home." Faith, by contrast, not only enables us to praise God but simultaneously floods our life with meaning and a sense of direction.

The identity question has always plagued the human spirit. Today perhaps we are even more sensitive to this question of "who are we" because of the growth and insights found in the field of psychology. I propose that one of the central elements of a religious identity is that *we are singers.* If God in fidelity calls us to intimacy, if a person of faith experientially participates in this reality, he or she breaks necessarily into song. We are born to sing; we were made to worship. Our identity as worshippers helps us to center our lives on what is essential. To identify with anything or anyone else than God is not only to be out of tune but to become ignorant of our being. An ancient singer invites us to song:

> Sing Yahweh a new song!
> Sing to Yahweh, all the earth!
> Sing to Yahweh, bless His name.
> Proclaim his salvation day after day,
> Tell of his glory among the nations,
> Tell his marvels to every people (Ps 96:1-2).

Perspective B: From Sharing to Adoption

The reality of love is constantly characterized by sharing. One expression of God's fidelity takes on visibility in that he has shared his very being and life in the marvel of creation. God is a giver: a giver of life, a giver of hope, a giver of holiness. Nothing comes into being or exists without his sustaining presence. It is difficult to get in touch with the depth of this reality. In contemplating the wonder of creation, we can easily agree with Emerson that "the reality is more excellent than the report." The report found in the first chapters of Genesis attempts to draw us into the mystery of God's gratuity. Whatever is, is only because God stands behind its being.

The immediate implication of this truth contains miles of ramifications; one, the mystery of creaturehood: all is created, made by a living and loving God. Facing this fact of being created prevents the not-so-infrequent danger of self-deification. Chesterton's wit drives home the point, "A great man knows he is not God, and the greater he is the better he knows it." Far from being a god, a person is God's handiwork. This creatureliness implies a radical dependency upon God for everything. An experience of this truth, moving from the "notional"

N. B.

(intellectualizing, theologizing) to the "real" (concrete experience), would transform our lives. Creatureliness means that we are essentially poor and that we stand with open hands before our God. Consoling, too, is the complementary truth: at all times we are being gifted with life, breath and every good thing. Fr. Orsy points out the relationship between our poverty and giftedness: "Who then is a person who is poor in his heart? The answer is that a poor person is one who lives on gifts, and gives away what he has. He relies on the goodness of others, but he does not make a collection of the gifts received" (*Open to the Spirit*, 113).

A God who shares his life and love and who calls mankind into existence is undoubtedly entitled to a response. Even a small child, possessing only a modicum of awareness, tends to respond to graciousness in various forms of gratitude, though perhaps the emphasis will be more on the gift than the giver. For the mature, the focus is on the thank you, centering on the person behind the gift. Gradually we come to realize that the thrill of receiving lies much more in the motive of love with which the gift is offered than in the tangible form of the gift itself. So, too, for the religious person; the realization of the personal, affective love of a caring God permeates the gift to such an extent that the gift itself becomes secondary. The focus rests on the gaze of the beloved. Then, joining the praise arising from God's fidelity, thanksgiving also becomes a way of life.

The Response of Gratitude. As faith disposes one to praise, a deep sense of gratitude enables a generous and spontaneous act of thanksgiving to spring forth from the human heart. Gratitude becomes a stance of one's mind and heart. It is the attitude grounded in fact and the habitual virtue embedded in the spirit of the poor. This frame of mind can handle Emerson's provocative reflection, "We do not quite forgive a giver." Rather than struggling against the fear of being indebted, the grateful heart is overwhelmed by the blessings received for no apparent reason. Not only is there no need for forgiveness, there is positive joy in the face of this divine concern. Even this ability to be grateful and joyful is, like faith, another gift of God. Again we see that our very cooperation is premised on a given disposition; the very source of the ability to give thanks is rooted in God's life. Though freedom allows for non-cooperation and the possible choice of taking things for granted, the sensitive and open spirit *must* respond in gratitude.

Another dimension of identity results from a consciousness of a God who desires that we participate in his life through the gift of creaturehood. This identity flows naturally from the thanksgiving rooted in the spirit of gratitude. We come to know ourselves as members of God's family, sons and daughters of the Father, sisters and brothers of Christ, sharers in the Spirit. We have before us a theology of relationship grounded in the mystery of creation. There is no other way to self-knowledge than this relational context. Gradually we begin to discern an intimacy within the human family as we sense ever more deeply our bonding in spiritual relationships. C. H. Dodd reminds us, "Where many individuals share an experience so intimate as the 'partnership of the Son of God' there must be a very intimate unity among them." The experience of being created gives us a staggering sense of identity: we are dependent, contingent, fragile and poor, and yet loved into being. This mysterious paradox overwhelms us with awe and wonder, if not a little fear. I am created! To rejoice in this face is a sure sign of mental and spiritual health.

Perspective C: From Disappointment to Forgiveness

[For several themes in this section we are indebted to François Roustang, *Growth in the Spirit* (Mission, Kans.: Sheed Andrews & McMeel, 1966), and to George Aschenbrenner, "Forgiveness" (*Sisters Today*, December 1973).]

In Isa 5:1-7, God's word tells of a man who planted a vineyard. After much labor and care, and with reasonable expectations of a good harvest, the gardener is sadly disappointed in that his vines produce sour grapes. What more could he have done? Was he not faithful to his garden, or did he not share enough? Impossible! Something else has gone wrong.

The story gives us another vision of the living and true God: he is a God of expectation! Having blessed and gifted the people of the universe with every good thing, their sincere appreciation should naturally follow. It does not, and God reacts to our lack of gratitude. This is not strange for a God who is vitally interested in every moment of human existence. No deistic God is possible for people of deep faith. Dare we go even further and, using the inadequacy of human language, say that God is not only a God of expectation, but also one of disappointment? Rejected, ignored and even despised by us, does God's face remain unchanged? Granted that God's love is unconditional, yet does not God grieve over his beloved but sinful people? An eternally happy God, unaffected by use or abuse of human freedom, raises many difficult questions. Resolution here demands that if we are to see the Father, we must look to Jesus; Jesus was moved by the love and hatred of his brothers and sisters.

With the harsh reality of unrequited love, we confront the mystery of sinfulness. We speak here of a stance before God, basically one of living outside his presence. When this happens, we are vulnerable to any and every type of violence and destruction. To live apart from God is to venture into nothingness and meaninglessness. It is to abandon light and hope, joy and peace. God no longer has any vital influence on our thoughts or activity. We live as though he does not exist. Individual sinful acts are "merely" the natural consequence of this deeper attitudinal position. They are more symptomatic than causal; they are signs disguising a much deeper and more deadly cancer. To come into contact with our personal and collective sinfulness is to realize our need for redemption. Every person has sinned; we have all spent time apart from faith. Thus everyone stands in need of God's tender forgiveness and the power of his healing reconciliation. No exemptions here!

The Response to Evil. One of the most powerful and noble acts of the human spirit takes place in the confessing of our responsibility for evil arising from our misuse of freedom. Hawthorne's plea at the end of *The Scarlet Letter* underlines this insight: "Among many morals which press upon us from the poor minister's miserable experience, we put only this into a sentence:—Be true! Be true! Be true! Show freely to the world, if not your worst, yet some trait whereby the worst may be inferred." The ability to assume responsibility for both the good done and evil committed is vital to maturity and sanctity. How quickly the Lord is willing to extend his mercy to anyone evidencing true sorrow. The prodigal son's welcome home should be branded on our memories. Facing sin demands courage and honesty. Confessing brings us back into the sphere of truth. Though painful in its birth, confessing results in incomparable joy and peace because of regained integrity.

Faith disposes us to praise, and gratitude enables us to respond to our giftedness. It is the gift of humility which liberates the spirit from pretense, hypocrisy and lies. So desirous is the human spirit of coming off looking well, of saving face, that confession of guilt is more traumatic than usually supposed. Though the source of liberation, truth can be brutal. We stand in great need of humility since this virtue gives us entrance into truth, the truth that leads to freedom. Tempted as we are to flee him "down the nights and down the days," unwilling to recognize the full meaning of our unresponsiveness to God's overwhelming love, we must recognize that the chase is senseless. We cannot outrun the Father's love. The sooner we turn around (conversion), the sooner we will be embraced by his joy and peace. Jesus was humble of heart; participating in his humility, we come to the Father.

To be a singer and a son or daughter are happy moments. To be identified as a sinner is less consoling though no less accurate. We are exactly that: a sinful people standing in need of redemption. To escape such an identity would seem to be the case with at least the saints, but they would not have it so. On the contrary, sensing the disproportion between God's love and their own response (though to us their response was indeed magnanimous), their self-imposed identity as great sinners was accurate. The sense of sinfulness increases in proportion to growth in the knowledge of God's love. This is a dangerous adventure, but there is no other road to take. "Everyone of us lives only to journey further and further into the mountains" (C. S. Lewis). Paradoxes continue to surface: both fear and joy accompany the sense of who we are before the face of the Father.

Perspective D: From Extravagance to Fellowship

In human interaction there would be little surprise if, after betrayal, a relationship would terminate in bitterness and resentment. Such a situation is quite comprehensible. Surprise of an authentic nature arises when we stand in the revelation of our triune God's response to our sinfulness. Language falters in describing God's response. One word attempts to capture the depth of the love: extravagance. Our God is extravagant in his concern; so unconditional is it that even our hatred and rejection cannot prevent God's coming back into human history in a totally new way. Cardinal Newman's description of the extravagance of human love might be applied analogously to God:

> I would not give much for that love which is never extravagant, which always observes the proprieties. . . . What mother, what husband or wife, what youth or maiden in love, but says a thousand foolish things, in a way of endearment, which the speaker would be sorry for strangers to hear; yet they are not on that account unwelcome to the parties to whom they are addressed.

God does not observe the proprieties. In the face of sin, he comes to us; what greater proof is needed of his love?

God's extravagance is no nebulous or abstract reality; it has visibility. The Father sent his only Son to reconcile all creation to himself. The mystery of the incarnation is so incredible that it verges on being scandalous. That God would and could become man! That he would do this through Mary in the mystery of the annunciation! That he would live in hiddenness, witness in the narrowness of time and space, undergo suffering and death, astound the world by his resurrection and ascension! The mystery of Jesus surpasses our wildest imagination. How marvelously God accommodates his revelation to our need of a story and the truth:

> [Christianity] met the mythological search for romance by being a story and the philosophical search for truth by being a true story . . . otherwise the two sides of the human mind could never have been touched at all; and the brain of man would have remained cloven and double; one lobe of it dreaming impossible dreams and the other repeating invariable calculations (G. K. Chesterton).

The Response of Discipleship. Following Christ, putting on his mind and heart, is the response to which we are invited. But this invitation to discipleship is no easy task. Following it means to enter into the paschal mystery and to gaze always at the beloved and attempt to share his peace and love with the world. This process of dying to self requires sacrifice and commitment; the recentering of our lives on the person of Jesus demands asceticism and surrender. Consoling for us is the fact that the footprints to the cross have already been made and we need but follow. More consoling is the glory of the resurrection assured us in the risen Lord. Our mission is to follow in our times and place the call of the Father.

The following and imitation of Christ is no nebulous, abstract happening. Rather, it is concrete and exacting, particular and exciting. The underlying disposition enabling such a response is that of surrender: the willingness to give not merely material things or even talents or time, but the offering of one's very person to the Lord, to do as he wills. What is at stake is the gift of freedom in obedience to the Father. The paradoxical nature of Christianity again surfaces: we gain our freedom only in its surrender. Further, the very source of liberation and ability to make this awesome sacrifice is itself a grace. God frees us from the slavery of our freedom! No one could possibly surrender oneself without trust and confidence, the cousins of hope. Because of their presence, surrender becomes a joy.

God's extravagance in Jesus and our joyous following through surrender adds another dimension to our identity. Besides being songsters, sons/daughters and sinners, we come to realize that we are eternal students, sitting daily before the Christ of the Gospel to learn the meaning of life and history. And learn we must, for the depth of ignorance, especially in regard to the living and true God, is vast. Even some of the greatest minds of the Church, though brilliant compared to the average person, were keenly sensitive to their own intellectual poverty when faced with the reality of a Triune God. Aquinas is reputed to have compared his own work to mere straw in the light of the full truth of God. Even though we will always be wanting in comprehension as we strive to know our Lord, there are many blessings in being in the role of a student: the challenge and excitement of new discoveries, the hope for more light and peace, the transformation of our minds and hearts that comes from experiencing the Father's love. Like the disciples we sit and hear his voice and see his face; then we venture forth to share a new Spirit and to foster the coming of the *N. B.* Kingdom.

Perspective E: From Powerlessness to Service

In his *Cost of Discipleship*, Dietrich Bonhoeffer speaks about Jesus in terms of being in need of help:

> Jesus is looking for help, for he cannot do the work alone. Who will come forward to help him and work with him? Only God knows, and he must give them to his Son. No man dare presume to come forward and offer himself on his own initiative, not even the disciples themselves. Their duty is to pray the Lord of the harvest to send forth labourers at the right moment, for the time is ripe.

Is it possible that God has deliberately put himself in the position of powerlessness? Could he not bring about the salvation of the whole world simply by exerting his infinite power? Does our God go so far as to make himself and his plan *dependent* upon human response? Scripture leaves no doubt that God wants (needs) co-workers, ambassadors to continue the work of the incarnation. God continues to look to mankind to make visible in every period of history his love and peace and joy. God counts on us to participate in sharing his life. Needless to say, this participation implies accountability (stewardship).

Two important mysteries of faith emerge in speaking about God in these terms. The first mystery deals with an enemy within existence. The Gospels often present Jesus speaking of an opponent to the Kingdom and indicating what signs accompany the presence of evil. "The Holy Ghost over the *bent* world broods . . ." points to the fact that all is not well. Weeds have been planted among the fields of wheat. Just below and beyond the placid and not so placid exterior of life, a fierce battle is being waged. The stakes are high—eternal destinies. God looks for warriors to engage the opponent and to fight evil in all its devious forms. Ultimate victory is assured in the light of a second mystery: the gift of God's Spirit enabling us to be fit instruments in the building up of the Church. The Pentecost event transforms the weak, heals the dispirited, energizes the inept. God's promise is realized in continuing his saving presence through the gift of the Spirit. Christian life demands that both of these mysteries be understood and responded to in proper ways.

The Response of Service. To experience the love of the Father in Jesus and to acknowledge that the Spirit is the first gift to all believers lead to a natural consequence: a desire to serve. Service is at the core of discipleship in that it is love made visible. The disciple readily and generously volunteers to be sent wherever the message of the good news needs to be seen and heard. The commission is a privilege, not a burden; it is a joy, not a restraint. This "being sent" is very personal. The experience of "Much Afraid" in Hannah Hurnard's *Hinds' Feet on High Places* speaks to the point: "To this place she was in the habit of going very early every morning to meet Him and learn His wishes and commands for the day, and again in the evening to give her report on the day's work." Serving under these circumstances becomes a way of life, and ministry, regardless of the cost, is essentially delightful. To be successful as a human being, service is necessary. Could absence of this facet of life foster the type of fortyish feeling described by E. M. Forster?

> Lovely, exquisite moment (gazing at the hills)—but passing the Englishman with averted face and on swift wings. He experienced nothing himself; it was as if someone had told him there was such a moment, and he was obliged to believe. And he felt dubious and discontented suddenly, and wondered whether he was really and truly successful as a human being. After forty years' experience, he had learnt to manage his life and make the best of it on advanced European lines, had developed his personality, explored his limitations, controlled his passions—and he had done it all without becoming either pedantic or worldly. A creditable achievement, but as the moment passed, he felt he ought to have been working at something else the whole time—he didn't know at what, never would know, never could know, and that was why he felt sad.

The wellspring of service is the gift of love enabling us to be "for" others. Where love is present, it becomes impossible to pass by a fellow pilgrim who is in need. Love appropriated results in deep conversion: a turning from self toward God and neighbor. St. Paul's conversion experience arose from the "peak experience" of discovering himself loved by the Father in Christ. Then all was new! This knowledge and love led the apostle of the Gentiles into the land of freedom, the field of service, the garden of joy and suffering. Being loved he became a lover of God and his people. Having been loved back into life, we also are to be gifts to others in sharing the Spirit. The prophet Isaiah speaks of the love covenant to which we are invited: "Pay attention, come to me; listen and your soul will live. With you I will make an everlasting covenant out of the favors promised to David" (55:3). This covenant liberates the human spirit from every form of oppression and enables the wounded to be healed and the separated to be united through love.

Our Christian identity states that we are worshippers, members of God's family, repentant sinners, disciples of the Lord. To this, a fifth element is now added: we are also servants! A servant is one commissioned both to *do* a joy and *"be* a gift and a benediction." Twentieth-century man and woman sense an uneasiness in this appellation. Much more acceptable would be the identity of leader, innovator or creative genius. Yet some of the great people of God—leaders, innovators and creative geniuses—all preferred the title servant: "From Paul, a servant of Christ Jesus who has been called to be apostle" (Romans 1:1). "Behold, O Lord, you are 'my king and my God.' Grant that whatsoever useful thing I learned as a child may be put to your service" (Augustine). "May it please his Majesty that we be worthy to do him some service, unmarred by the many faults that we always commit, even in doing our good works!" (Teresa of Avila)

A servant takes a fundamental stance before God: a stance of openness, of being moved by the Spirit, of surrendering to the divine will. Though the initiative is always from God, this is no passive position. Once listening (obedience) is done in silence and solitude, the servant assumes responsibility and must fulfill the mission. Jesus was sent; he served his Father. Surprising, perhaps, is the realization that there is no real choice in life other than serving; choice is simply what or who is served. Choices range from serving one's ego (seeking power, status, wealth) to doing the work of the Lord. Servants all, but energy and time and love channeled in divers directions. We are called to serve. In this is much of our joy and hope.

3

Presence and Poetry
Healing Power in Poetry

Emerson, gifted with the skill of conciseness, states, "The first wealth is health."[1] Our poverty, therefore, flows from our illness of body, psyche, and soul. It was into a world of radical deprivation that Jesus came to bring to us the fulness of life. He came to heal, to restore, to free, and to reconcile. Behind his gracious words and bold action was the great healing poem of love, a love that transformed crippled bodies, anguished minds, darkened spirits. The music of this poem continues to ring out in the lives of those who are his followers. Whoever is touched by the sound of the good news, God's love and forgiveness, regains the path of health and newness of life.

The thesis of this article is that poetry has within it the power to heal the human spirit. Obviously, this will be poetry of a special nature, though not necessarily what might be called faith poetry, poetry that is either implicitly or explicitly centered on God. All authentic poetry touches in some way on Truth, Goodness and Beauty, and it is precisely in this that life comes to the human spirit.

More directly, I would like to suggest that poetry's music heals for five reasons: because it is incarnational it draws us into contact with reality; because of its emotive and imaginative power it touches the heart; because it interprets and provides vision it expands the mind; because it provides companionship it helps us deal with loneliness; because it demands silence it points the way to wisdom. Before attempting to demonstrate these points, some reflections on the notion of health are in order.

The Wealth of Health

At bottom, health is lost by being out of touch. Lewis Thomas, in speaking about the tiny termite, observes a fact that, when applied analogously to humans, has radical significance: "It is the being touched that counts, rather than the act of touching. Deprived of antennae, any termite can become a group termite if touched enough by the others."[2]

When the body is deprived of proper nutrition, it weakens and becomes ill; when people, through the various forms of discrimination and segregation, are deprived of just associations, they languish and die within; when the human soul is parted from God through sin, darkness and fear penetrate the spirit.

The causes of illness are legion: negligence, misused freedom, prejudice, bigotry, selfishness, hostility, apathy. A considerable amount of contemporary emotional and spiritual illness might well be traced to the philosophers of utilitarianism:

> They became first introspective and then introverted; cut off from their fellows as they were, they became secretive and sometimes neurotic. It should surprise no one that vast areas of contemporary art employ a private language, insist upon subjectivity, deliberately refuse to communicate. The man to whom no one speaks is the man most likely to fall sick.[3]

If certain substances, actions and fundamental options cause illness, the reverse is also true: substances, actions, and options of a different nature promote health and well-being. It was the search for the latter that led Macbeth to say:

> Cure her of that:
> Canst thou not minister to a mind diseas'd,
> Pluck from the memory a rooted sorrow,
> Raze out the written troubles of the brain,
> And with some sweet oblivious antidote
> Cleanse the stuff'd bosom of that perilous stuff
> Which weighs upon the heart? (Act V, Sc. iii)

Where do we find that "sweet oblivious antidote"? One possible alternative, though perhaps in the troubled soul of Lady Macbeth a futile option, would be poetry. As a means to health, poems touch the deepest recesses of our hearts, calling us to live in close proximity to the finite world, while simultaneously opening us to the infinite. Dr. Félix Martí-Ibáñez, in writing about the Hindu preacher Vivekananda, states, "For him God was the First Poet, and the universe and its creatures were His finest poems."[4]

Through both the written and creature-poems we come to the Poet, the source of all life and holiness. The union that poetry fosters is crucial to health. Karl Rahner writes powerfully of the poet's interiority and the necessity that the poet write from a deep withinness:

> According to Goethe, to the true poet "a God has given the mission to say what he suffers"—while others remain dumb in their agony and in their happiness. The poet has the happy but also dangerous—overwhelmingly dangerous—pleasure of the aesthetic identity between his being and his consciousness. He attains that "coming to his self" and "being with himself" which Thomas calls the *reditio completa in se ipsum.* . . .
>
> The poet experiences this in the pictorial concreteness of the fresh and pregnant poetic statement, wherein all is contained at once: spirit and body, nearness and distance, the infinitely profound and the childishly intelligible. Ah, this is a sublime happiness: to be so reconciled with oneself, so near oneself, so close to one's own infinite distance; to be able to understand oneself in that one says himself, even when he seems to be talking about something entirely different.[5]

What happens in the creative process for the poet, a striving toward wholeness and health in deep self-knowledge, can happen vicariously to the reader of poetry who enters into the shared experience. And where there is wholeness, holiness is near at hand.

An illustration of the healing power of poetry is contained in Walter Kerr's *The Decline of Pleasure.* At the age of twenty-one, John Stuart Mill had a mental breakdown. Pressured by his father into a program of intensive study with emphasis on strictly analytic thought, Mill was unable to cope and became ill. Kerr writes:

> He now saw, he reported in his autobiography, "that the habit of analysis has a tendency to wear away the feelings . . . when no other mental habit is cultivated," and "the maintenance of a due balance among the faculties" became for him a matter of urgent importance. Unexpectedly, it was poetry that had most helped him recover his joy in life:
>
> "What made Wordsworth's poems a medicine for my state of mind, was that they expressed, not mere outward beauty, but states of feeling, and of thought coloured by feeling, under the excitement of beauty. . . . In them I seemed to draw from a source of inward

joy, of sympathetic and imaginative pleasure, which could be shared in by all human beings. . . . I needed to be made to feel that there was real, permanent happiness in tranquil contemplation. Wordsworth taught me this. . . . The result was that I gradually, but completely, emerged from my habitual depression, and was never again subject to it."[6]

Poetry's power lies in its ability to integrate our emotions with the rest of life. A culture which represses feelings puts an undue strain on the human psyche. Just as our intellects pursue a solid philosophy and theology, just as our energies seek expression in external achievement, so feelings strive toward actualization, and poetry can often be a healthy means. Mill came to healing through the gentle stirrings of his feelings touched by the beauty of a poetic world.

Simone Weil, the fascinating but enigmatic figure of our own century, was keenly aware of the need for poetry among the workers whose lives she shared. Poetry for her was grounded in religion and provided an opening for moments and experiences of transcendence. She penned this strong statement: "Workers need poetry more than bread. They need that their life should be a poem. They need some light from eternity. Religion alone can be the source of such poetry. It is not religion but revolution which is the opium of the people."[7]

Another French author, Raïssa Maritain, expresses a similar thought: "Only theology and poetry can speak of God. Knowledge, inspiration and experience."[8] The implications here are multiple. Without poetry, vision and life are endangered. Without poetry, the outer agenda of work, activism, and productivity tend to become all-consuming. Without poetry, we close a major arterial on the path to God.

The First Reason for Poetry's Healing Power

Poetry is essentially incarnational. The human person is a composite of many ingredients: intellect, imagination, will, body. Communication and life take on full meaning only to the degree that all aspects of the human person are adequately dealt with. The old scholastic adage contains an eternal pearl of wisdom: "no idea without its phantasm." A person is no abstract intellect seeking only meaning, nor sheer imagination being stirred to delight by beauty and strong affectivity. Ideas and feelings, the good and the pleasurable—all blend to attract us and hold our attention.

Poetry incarnates life's experiences by articulating them in profound insights, concrete images, stirring rhythm, and specific choices.

Poetry enfleshes for the whole person wisdom carefully ferreted out from confusing underbrush; poetry provides warmth and texture in otherwise drab encounters; poetry draws the heart to tender and joyous responses. What the poet is about is magnificently described by Joseph Conrad:

> To arrest, for the space of a breath, the hands busy about the work of the earth, and compel men entranced by the sight of distant goals to glance for a moment at the surrounding vision of form and color, of sunshine and shadows; to make them pause for a look, for a sigh, for a smile—such is the aim, difficult and evanescent, and reserved only for a very few to achieve. But sometimes, by the deserving and the fortunate, even that task is accomplished. And when it is accomplished—behold!—all the truth of life is there: a moment of vision, a sign, a smile—and the return to an eternal rest.[9]

Why does such a moment described by Conrad heal? Ancient philosophers often stated that we were born to see. Vision of the truth, by its very nature, heals even if initially it causes pain; a sigh, that mysterious human utterance surfacing from a depth seldom known, draws us into reality with such force that we begin to surmise that the goal of life is not external but within; a smile, that curious non-verbal happiness, means that we have, however momentarily, sneaked up on creation and seen it in its pristine beauty.

Because the poet has seen and sighed and smiled, because he has been captivated by reality and lost in its wonderment, he is now able to provide a vision, skillfully articulating his experience for others.

In the Christian context, the most profound reality made visible to history is the mystery of the incarnation. The enfleshment of God's love in Jesus is *the* poem, and the very process of making explicit what is implicit lies at the heart of poetry. A poem embodies what otherwise might well go unnoticed, thus unpraised and unappreciated.

C. S. Lewis shows the interrelationship among Christianity, the incarnation, and poetry:

> [The Incarnation, for instance,] far from denying what we already know of reality, writes the comment which makes the crabbed text plain; or rather, proves itself to be the text on which Nature was only the commentary. In science we have been reading only the notes to a poem; in Christianity we find the poem itself.[10]

Science, always limited by its method and objectivity, cannot penetrate into the heart of things, their interiority. The world of love is a stranger to science. Poetry, however, plunges into the central mysteries of life, particularly the mystery of love. Unconcerned about empirical verification and exactitude of objective discourse, the poet moves in the land of mystery, wonder and ah-ness. In faith, the Christian sees the incarnation as the deepest poetic expression of love. Healing takes place here because the mystery and wonder of Jesus becoming human provide the vision and love necessary for health.

John of the Cross, in his poetic *Spiritual Canticle,* describes how the incarnation promotes our happiness, and thus our health:

> . . . to see Him face to face and thoroughly understand the profound and eternal mysteries of His Incarnation . . . is by no means the lesser part of beatitude. As Christ Himself says to the Father in St. John's Gospel: "This is eternal life, that they might know You, the one true God and Your Son Jesus Christ, Whom You have sent" (John 17:3). The first thing a person desires to do after having come a long distance is to see and converse with the one he deeply loves; similarly, the first thing the soul desires upon coming to the vision of God is to know and enjoy the deep secrets and mysteries of the Incarnation and the ancient ways of God dependent upon it.[11]

Just as Christ healed by making love visible, so a poem gives flesh and blood to those forces (vision, joy, insight, passion, tenderness) that enrich and restore the human spirit. The incarnation itself is the archetype for all life-giving poetry.

The Second Reason for Poetry's Healing Power

Poetry comes from the heart and touches the heart. Whether or not the Little Prince was philosophically correct in suggesting that what is essential is invisible to the eye and that it is only with the heart that one sees rightly, we all know from experience that affectivity, symbolized by the heart, plays a predominant and central role in human experience. The language of the heart is the language of poetry: heart speaking to heart (*cor ad cor*).

Poetry's emotive force is the affections; from this wellspring the poem enters into the hearts of others, stirring and moving people to action and experience. The roots of health lie within the heart, and when the heart is touched (and this is one of the chief aims of poetry) health is not far behind.

This touching can happen only insofar as the poem comes from the depths, a heart experience: "For one can be a poet only when the word of the mouth breaks forth from the center of the heart. The poet says that which he bears within him. He expresses himself in truth."[12]

The truth of poetry cannot be compared with the "hard" truth of other disciplines. Poetry's truth is colored and immersed in love and respect; it is precisely this reverential atmosphere of truth flowing from the heart that allows that same truth to be received into the heart of another, regardless of the sacrifice, pain, or challenge. Healing prospers in the presence of affective truth and truthful affection; indeed, in the presence of a poem.

Gerard Manley Hopkins' "God's Grandeur" serves as an illustration of a poem that comes from the heart and touches the heart. The poem has three stages: (1) a powerful reflection on how all of creation is charged with the glory and grandeur of God, brilliantly described in flashing verbs and majestic images; (2) an insightful and anguished gaze at human plodding and gross insensitivity; (3) a hope-filled and courageous vision that, despite human irreverence, creation is yet permeated with a "dearest freshness" because God's Spirit broods over the bent but not broken world.

Although this poem is not devoid of profound truth and a rich theology, it is the reader's heart that is touched. The thrill and glory of such magnificent beauty, the horrible and incredible blinding and stupidity of historical man, the fidelity and tenderness of God despite human response: all stir the heart to a variety of feelings and responses. How deeply Hopkins' heart was touched! How deeply his words touch our lives in this marvelous piece of literature!

The center of hell for Dante is a frozen lake; the center of illness is a hardened heart, a real hell. A heart unable to enter into poetic experiences is in danger. And yet, even the most hardened heart, when exposed however unwillingly to the reverence and power of strong, gentle words (E. Scrooge excepted), becomes vulnerable to life.

As a resisting patient is unable to stop the healing effect of an injection, so the insensitive becomes susceptible to the heart language of poetry. It may well take years, even decades, but eventually poetry will have its results. Though a generous disposition would be preferable, the human condition being what it is, poetry must at times struggle on the field of hostile territory. Only after having made a risky entrance might it become a welcomed, perhaps even a longed-for guest. Delightful medicine here to ward off future hardness and insensitivity.

Fulness of life and health knows little about moderation. The intellect tends to draw boundaries and calculate too exactly; 'tis the heart that flies free and is extravagant:

Saints have no moderation,
nor do poets,
just exuberance.[13]

The Third Reason for Poetry's Healing Power

Poetry interprets experience. Theologians and philosophers find it possible to discourse on topics foreign to their experience: the eschaton, angels, nothingness, prime matter. Poets must write from experience. Yet, experience in and of itself does not provide nourishment for the human spirit; it must be interpreted.

The adage that "experiences unreflected upon dehumanize" contains much truth. Poems are experiences tasted and shared. From the point of view of health, the human spirit becomes ill when deprived of meaning; with meaning, life becomes significant and imbued with enthusiasm.

The poets offer insight into many universal questions which demand some insight: the possibility of love, the fear of death, the anguish of suffering, the problem of God, the meaning of existence. Poets not only recognize the questions but provide some form of interpretation of life's experiences, thus enabling the person to search out and find some personal significance.

Form is not sufficient; content containing a message is also demanded. Chesterton saw the need for this dimension of meaning: "And poetry without philosophy has only inspiration, or, in vulgar language, only wind." Poetry must involve reality therapy; it puts us in contact with the truth. In the end, however long the journey and despite the pain, truth heals. Poetry that speaks the truth frees and strengthens; it enlightens, enkindles, and enables.

In a special way, faith poetry, poetry that interprets reality in terms of the God experience, brings fuller light and life into the human spirit. Contemplation here is a wellspring of spiritual growth. Some of the great classical literature in spirituality is simply a commentary on faith poetry.

The interpretation of experience which provides meaning comes in a certain form of language—the language of images. Through the visibility and sensibility of images, contact is made with reality. Language here is almost as universal as music, for in images we are dynamically reconnected with things; we are grounded in reality.

The following poem combines images, experiences, and meaning in sharing a vision:

```
 . . . that the steps I walk
         whether in this city
                 another city
                 another state          be His footprints,
 . . . that the thoughts I dream
         whether in an office
                 a classroom
                 a car                  be His ideas,
 . . . that the moves I make
         whether behind a camera
                     a typewriter
                     a book             be His hands,
 . . . that the words I say
         whether to a stranger
                 a co-worker
                 a friend               be His message,
 . . . that the person I am
         whether as a religious
                 or as a lay woman      be His image.
```

Please pray with me
  for I cannot "become"
  alone,
and He has given me much
  that is to be shared.
    How
    Where
    When only God knows.
But, I would ask you
  to stay with me
    on the way
    to finding out.[14]

This poem heals because it integrates. By bringing together the many, varied human activities under a single unifying principle—the desire to live in union with Christ—the poem shares a meaningful message. Health comes in relationships; the deepest health and life come in our living in Jesus. Thus the concluding call and the need for support provide insight into a basic question of our spiritual journey.

The Fourth Reason for Poetry's Healing Power

Poetry provides companionship. Poets see and share. In this exists companionship, the breaking of bread which nourishes and sustains. Over the centuries the poets have been joined by vast throngs. Homer and Dante, Virgil and Milton, Shelley and Keats have walked few miles alone. But who calls whom? As Dr. Félix Martí-Ibáñez writes:

> Every man goes through life shielding his individual smallness behind a majestic group of giants whom he chooses as life companions. This august and mighty troupe is acquired sometimes all at once, sometimes in the course of years. The choice of such peerless companions is made because their personality charms us, their life inspires us, or their word enlightens us. Sometimes we have had the good fortune to know them personally; most often we come to know them through their work, their speeches, writing, thoughts and example. But maybe it is not we who choose them to accompany us on life's journey; maybe it is they who from their exalted place reach down to adopt us, even as the sun in its journey across the heavens chooses to mirror itself in the humble water of a brooklet.[15]

Through the companionship offered by poetry, various maladies plaguing the human spirit are dealt with. The anguish and distress of loneliness are alleviated when poems allow us to experience the fact that our apparently singular feelings, thoughts, or conduct are much more universal than previously considered. In the kindred soul of the poet our own experience is validated if not confirmed. Such empathy and implicit compassion heal by their very nature.

In "The Poison Tree" William Blake shares an experience of anger. When anger is dealt with directly and is properly claimed, it comes to an end; when it is repressed and denied, it becomes poisonous. This universal experience of anger as dealt with in the eighteenth century speaks to the twentieth-century pilgrim with great force and accuracy.

Tennyson writes of how a single flower, if understood totally, would give us knowledge of God and man.[16] Our search for meaning in our own times might well take a lesson here: it is not through acquiring vast knowledge that one achieves wisdom and insight, but in deepening one's understanding of the meaning of life.

The poets heal by allowing us to identify with their experiences and learn from their insights—fitting companions, indeed. Such authentic sharing gives life by restoring a desolate spirit, enriching a languishing mind, inspiring an apathetic will, confirming movements of the heart. Dante's pilgrimage with Virgil is the paradigm for any of us who look to the poets for companionship.

Intrinsic to any real companionship is the note, so pleasant to the ears yet seldom heard these days, of foreverness. True companions journey faithfully through all kinds of experiences, be they life or death, peace or anguish, light or dark. Companionship is not selective; the whole of existence is embraced, felt, examined, and lived. Health flows from such fidelity and mutuality. Poems that have worked their way into our hearts (and have gotten stuck there) are lifelong friends; and with those gifts dwells the giver.

The Fifth Reason for Poetry's Healing Power

Poetry's music fosters silence. Carl Sandburg has written, "In perfect silence there is music." Whether or not the opposite is true, that in music there lies a mysterious silence, is open to conjecture. Whatever the case, there is no poetry without music and silence. Nor is there health in life without some quality of silence and probably a good portion of music.

The poet encounters reality at a depth level and, like a deep sea diver, finds an enormous and awesome silence in these regions. Disciplined silence is a part of the creative process; stillness within is a prerequisite for seeing and hearing. Herein lies the best poetry, "for the best poetry is not in spoken words; the best poetry is in what man's soul experiences when he is listening to his inner song, a song that has no words."[17] Indeed, life is instrumental before it becomes lyrical.

The sensitive reader of poetry is drawn into the healing silence which alone allows for dialogue. From that quiet song and reverential silence the poet speaks; in tender silence the listener receives the poet's gift which then moves the mind and heart into the frequency of a new song. Health is restored in this miracle of dialogue, person speaking to person, heart to heart. Such bonding and unity enrich life. The nutrients of poetry (silence, music, dialogue, and receptivity) enable the discerning reader to achieve mature growth. And what a delightful balance the gift of poetry brings!

Health is fostered by moving from self-knowledge to self-understanding to self-acceptance and finally to self-transcendence. Being pulled out of ourselves and getting lost in a healthy human experience is important for the quality of life. The self-transcendence that music works in us is called ecstasy; the music contained in poetry is ecstatic.

Poetry draws us into wider horizons, allowing us to taste experiences otherwise banned from our narrow, introspective consciousness. Through the door of music and poetry we enter into fuller reality and begin to touch the very origin (and destiny) of being. From silence and in song, Tennyson's poem "Flower in the Crannied Wall" takes us to that source and goal:

> Flower in the crannied wall,
> I pluck you out of the crannies.
> I hold you here, root and all, in my hand,
> Little flower—but *if* I could understand
> What you are, root and all, and all in all,
> I should know what God and man is.

Health has another popular name: integration. When all parts are working as a harmonious whole, when all elements function in congruence, when each relationship respects all others, there is a healthy (whole) and holy situation. The opposite is also true: disintegration of parts, elements, relationships leads to illness, possibly death.

St. Paul, in writing to the Philippians, challenges his fellow Christians to integration and health. His call is to appreciate whatever is true, good, and beautiful, and in doing this to find God, the origin of life and health. His poetic message is striking:

> Finally, brothers, fill your minds with everything that is true, everything that is noble, everything that is good and pure, everything that we love and honour, and everything that can be thought virtuous or worthy of praise. Keep doing all the things that you learnt from me and have been taught by me and have heard or seen that I do. Then the God of peace will be with you (4:8-9).

What St. Paul spoke in the first century George Herbert echoed in the seventeenth century. In a concise and thought-filled poem, "Trinity Sunday," the voice of the poet challenges us to integration: that we realize the source of our creaturehood, redemption and sanctification; recognize the mystery of sin and its destructive energies; invoke the source of life for necessary enrichment; respond by being willing to journey with God.

> Lord, who has form'd me out of mud,
>   And has redeem'd me through thy blood,
>   And sanctifi'd me to do good;
> Purge all my sins done heretofore:
>   For I confess my heavy score,
>   And I will strive to sin no more.
> Enrich my heart, mouth, hands in me,
>   With faith, with hope, with charity;
>   That I may run, rise, rest with thee.

Ultimately, as Christians, we rest in the Poet, our God, whose poem we are, however unrhythmical, however unharmonious, however resistant. The Poet continues to fashion us, for we are as yet incomplete. Our health is never gained once and for all; there are always unredeemed areas of our hearts seeking healing.

One remedy that soothes and consoles is the gift of poetry, a gift that ultimately comes from God but does so through a variety of personal intermediaries. In poetry we gain health because it meets the basic needs of the human spirit and thereby fosters the kingdom. A contemporary author writes:

> If we are to ascertain the success or failure of Christianity, we must know exactly what the mission of Christ is. His mission is twofold: to show forth the Father and to unite us with the Godhead. In this way he satisfies man's twofold basic human need for intuition and for vital union. A man loves to see, admire, and contemplate good, beautiful things; he also loves to become in some way equated or identified with them. Thus you have always in the face of the true, the good, and the beautiful (wine, food, music, a woman, a man) the need for intuition and union. The mission of Christianity, therefore, is to enable man to see God and to be with God.[18]

The poet and his or her poem have the same basic mission: to offer the possibility of health and life to the full.

1. "Power," *Essays of Ralph Waldo Emerson* (New York: The Book League of America, 1941) 383.

2. Lewis Thomas, *The Lives of a Cell: Notes of a Biology Watcher* (New York: Bantam Books, Inc., 1974) 62–63.

3. Walter Kerr, *The Decline of Pleasure* (New York: Simon & Schuster, Inc., 1962) 77.

4. Félix Martí-Ibáñez, *The Crystal Arrow* (New York: Clarkson N. Potter, Inc., 1964) 25.

5. Karl Rahner, "Priest and Poet," 4–5. Source unknown.

6. Kerr, *The Decline of Pleasure* 54–55.

7. *The Simone Weil Reader*, ed. George A. Panichas (New York: David McKay Co., Inc., 1977) 120.

8. *Raïssa's Journal*, presented by Jacques Maritain (Albany, N.Y.: Magi Books, Inc., 1963) 328.

9. Joseph Conrad, *The Nigger of the Narcissus* (New York: Dell Publishing Co., Inc., 1960) 29.

10. Roger Lancelyn Green and Walter Hooper, *C. S. Lewis: A Biography* (New York: Harcourt Brace Jovanovich, Inc., 1974) 227.

11. *The Collected Works of St. John of the Cross*, trans. Kieran Kavanaugh, O.C.D., and Otilio Rodríguez, O.C.D. (ICS Publications, Institute of Carmelite Studies, Washington, 1973) 550.

12. Rahner, "Priest and Poet" 16.

13. Anne Sexton, *The Awful Rowing Toward God* (Boston: Houghton Mifflin Co., 1975) 81.

14. Barbara Holt, "Please Pray With Me."

15. Martí-Ibáñez, *The Crystal Arrow* 17.

16. Alfred Lord Tennyson, "Flower in the Crannied Wall."

17. Martí-Ibáñez, *The Crystal Arrow* xv.

18. William McNamara, *The Human Adventure* (New York: Doubleday & Co., Inc., 1976) 188.

4

Presence and Praise
Divine Host and Hesitant Guest in George Herbert's Poem "Love"

In the following poem George Herbert, a seventeenth-century Anglican clergyman, shares with us his deeply religious description of the God-human experience.

Love

Love bade me welcome; yet my soul drew back,
    Guilty of lust and sin.
But quick-eyed Love, observing me grow slack
    From my first entrance in,
Drew nearer to me, sweetly questioning,
    If I lacked anything.

"A guest," I answered, "worthy to be here."
    Love said, "You shall be he."
"I, the unkind, ungrateful? Ah, my dear,
    I cannot look on thee."
Love took my hand, and smiling did reply,
    "Who made the eyes but I?"

"Truth, Lord, but I have marred them; let my shame
    Go where it doth deserve."
"And know you not," says Love, "who bore the blame?"
    "My dear, then I will serve."
"You must sit down," says Love, "and taste my meat."
    So I did sit and eat.

At the age of thirty-nine George Herbert was dead. Ordained an Anglican priest only three years, this orator, poet and minister of God's word passed through the gate of death to experience directly his deepest desire, the living and true God. His legacy, available to anyone interested, is his profound but indirect experiences of God as the poet recorded these throughout his brief life's journey. Herbert's poems provide a source of inspiration and a stimulus for similar religious experiences for those who ponder the inner meaning and joy of his words. This chapter is a personal commentary on the above poem. Hopefully its subjectivity will not contradict the intrinsic meaning of the original experience.

My first contact with Herbert's poetry came from the reading of Simone Weil's *Waiting for God.* In her autobiographical writings Weil describes Herbert's influence on her life, especially his poem "Love":

> There was a young English Catholic there from whom I gained my first idea of the supernatural power of the sacraments because of the truly angelic radiance with which he seemed to be clothed after going to communion. Chance—for I always prefer saying chance rather than Providence—made of him a messenger to me. For he told me of the existence of those English poets of the seventeenth century who are named metaphysical. In reading them later on, I discovered the poem of which I read you what is unfortunately a very inadequate translation. It is called "Love." I learned it by heart. Often, at the culminating point of a violent headache, I make myself say it over, concentrating all my attention upon it and clinging with all my soul to the tenderness it enshrines. I used to think I was merely reciting it as a beautiful poem, but without knowing it the recitation had the virtue of a prayer. It was during one of these recitations that, as I told you, Christ himself came down and took possession of me.[1]

In this account the universal creative process is at work. Herbert had come to experience God in a unique way in his personal life. After careful reflections and affective stirrings, gifted with the necessary technical and literary skills, he was able to articulate that deep mystical experience in verbal, poetic form. Weil, centuries later and living in a different culture, read the poem, was drawn back through its deep affections and insight, and experienced the same reality, a God of love and concern. What happened to Weil can happen to us. Our reverent reflection on faith poetry can be the inspiration for personal religious experience. The *sine qua non* is proper disposition. Given this, the shared experiences of others throughout history need not be lost; rather, we, in our time and place, can re-experience some precious and intimate moments of God's encounter with humankind. With this background and with a keen awareness of the dangers involved in dissecting a poem, we proceed to search out the implicit theology and tangible joy of Herbert's poem.

God: The Divine Host

A central consideration of any spirituality is one's concept or image of God. As the arrow's direction is determined for good or ill once it leaves the bow, so our spirituality is given direction in terms of our perception of who the living and true God really is. With fidelity to the Scriptures and with confidence in his own personal experience, Herbert conceives God as Love. The great significance of this is stressed by the title of the poem. Herbert's theological accuracy is confirmed in St. John's first epistle: "Anyone who fails to love can never have known God, because God is love" (4:8). Although we might tend to take this conception as normal, history presents many distorted images and illusions: a god of unconcern (deism), a god of hostility and caprice (mythologies), a god of questioned existence (forms of existentialism). Herbert's vision contests all such caricatures: the Christian God is one of concern, a God of fidelity, a God of life. Basic to Herbert's approach is an underlying disposition of reverence, awe and wonder. Without these qualities, God cannot be known. Chesterton and C. S. Lewis were keenly aware of the importance of attitude in approaching the Divine:

> This is the attitude of most paganism towards God. He is something assumed and forgotten and remembered by accident; a habit possibly not peculiar to pagans.[2]
>
> I had approached God, or my idea of God, without love, without awe, even without fear.[3]

Love bade me welcome. Love is dynamic. Its true and authentic nature is demonstrated by sharing and reaching out to others (more accurately we might say by drawing others into the gift of love). Thus God, the divinely gracious host, extends himself in hospitality by inviting this person, the potential guest, to enter into his presence. Present here is an entire theology which sees grace as basically the self-communication of God to a human person. God is a God who longs to be with his people; he desires that his people be always with him. God offers this covenant freely and he pitches his tent among men. Two dimensions of this loving God become clear: his rich fidelity and his profound intimacy.

The Host is sensitive to every stirring of the guest. Nothing escapes his gaze, especially the predominant tendency of humans to fear Truth, Goodness and Beauty. His love is quick-eyed, observing, recording and responding to the slightest and most secret movement of one's heart. God's gaze is creative in that it draws the guest, who is on the verge of flight, nearer to the mystery of love. Entering the range of God's love overwhelms the guest; indeed, one's very existence seems in jeopardy. The ambivalence at this moment is deep and perplexing. On the one side is trembling: "The mountains to their bases, and the seas, are shaken; the rocks, like wax, melt before your glance" (Jdt 16:18-19). On the other hand is consolation: ". . . you are precious in my eyes, because you are honored and I love you" (Isa 43:4). God's gaze both purifies and soothes.

An educational process goes on throughout the entire poem. Questions are continually raised and this pedagogical method, known as the Socratic method, is employed effectively. By means of questions, Socrates in his day attempted to prove to people their ignorance, a task at which he was very successful, as we see in Plato's dialogues. Though Socrates was without doubt a religious man and perhaps in his personal prayer experienced the method attributed to him in a certain way, we can detect in Herbert's poem a most fruitful and positive process of education which can be called the theistic method. The goal is not to prove to others their ignorance but, through careful and respectful questioning, lead them to the truth. Herbert presents God as a questioning, guiding God. Again the Scriptures validate this concept of God, for in Jesus, the visible image of the Father, we see a teacher who is continually questioning his disciples and the people: "Would you bring in a lamp to put it under a tub or under a bed?" (Mark 4:21) . . . "Why are you so frightened? How is it that you have no faith?" (Mark 4:40) . . . "What gain, then, is it for a man to win the whole world and ruin his life?" (Mark 8:36) . . . "What did Moses command you?" (Mark 10:3)

In teaching people through these haunting questions, the divine teacher caused reflection, evaluation, decision and responsibility to flourish as realities in the people he loved so dearly and whom he wanted to share in the fulness of life (John 10:10). Several profound questions are asked by Love (God) in the poem: 1) *If I lacked anything.* Though perhaps filled with many things on the sensory and intellectual levels, the implication is that the greatest need, spiritual communion, remains wanting. The question forces the guest into the paradox that without Love one lacks everything though possessing some things. St. Paul's famous hymn on love (1 Cor 13) exemplifies this point. A person with eloquence, prophecy and even generosity (gives all things to be burned) has "nothing" unless love is present. 2) *Who made the eyes but I?* What or who is the source of one's existence? Without the eye-I-ego we do not exist. Whence does it arise? What is the meaning of creaturehood, of being made? The challenge here is to look deeply into the cause of all being and to emerge from the journey with wisdom, realizing that all life, all holiness comes from God. Though this second question appears so simple, it is a metaphysical and cosmological question which, if left unanswered, causes futility and despair to reside in the human heart. 3) *Know you not who bore the blame?* This third question drives home the extent of God's precious and extravagant love. God is not only the maker of the eye, he not only fills up what is lacking in our being, but he has come among us as Savior to take upon himself our blame, the consequences of sins. This redemptive act is *the* expression of love which is symbolized so dramatically in the cross. Dying for another cannot be superseded. The weight of sin could be borne only by infinite love. This inescapable question corners us into facing a fundamental reality of our lives: we are sinners in need of redemption and this redemption has already been won for us through God's love, Christ the Lord.

Herbert's view of the Divine Host as a God of intimacy and a God who questions his people into the truth is supplemented by a third characteristic. God's pedagogy, the theistic method, moves beyond questions to make strong, declarative statements, especially when the response of the guest wanders from the truth. The invited guest, deeply conscious of his unworthiness, seeks to back off from the invitation. Indeed, he has good cause, his personal sinfulness. How common this pattern is throughout salvation history: Simon Peter, at the great catch of fish, falls to his knees before Jesus and says, "Leave me, Lord, for I am a sinful man" (Mark 5:1); St. Paul, having persecuted the church, states that he is unworthy to be called an apostle (1 Cor 15:9); Isaiah identifies himself as a man of unclean lips during his religious experience in the temple (6:5). Despite this, God's mercy and love are larger than human unworthiness. In the poem God's strong assertive statement sweeps aside the accurate but conquerable excuse of the guest and states, "You shall be he." If the Lord had to wait for a truly worthy guest, his house would remain eternally empty. God's predilection for the poor and sick remains constant.

A second instance of Love moving from questioning to assertion is present when the invited guest, queried about who bore the blame, knowing the answer, and hurriedly promising to serve, is confronted with a forceful command: "You must sit down and taste the meat." The Host, keenly aware of the defense mechanism of flight from encounter, uses an imperative to point to the truth. What is implicit here is the necessity of balance between activity and prayer, the apostolate and one's contemplative life. Service is important and necessary, but there is also a time for quiet presence and sharing. In this poem that time has come. The work (service) that is temporarily set aside will not disappear. However, after dwelling in Love's presence, we accomplish the tasks of life in the context of sharing that love with others.

The Hesitant Guest

Night and darkness are universal images depicting something about the nature of sin. Herbert had a profound insight into the reality of sinfulness and understood well the meaning of man's turning from God with the subsequent loss of vision. The poem speaks of lust and sin which, as we all know, cause healthy guilt in the heart of every reflective and sensitive person. Through parallel construction the poet associates lust with unkindness and sin with ingratitude, an association both psychologically and theologically sound. Unkindness results from turning people into objects; lust is essentially that process. Sexual exploitation is symbolic of that lack of charity which tears people apart, depriving them of their inherent dignity. Lust means lack of love; its presence in our lives makes it extremely embarrassing to approach Love himself. As Merton succinctly states, ". . . fear is inseparable from pride and lust."[4]

Ingratitude, a universal pattern of sin, means that we refuse to recognize reality for what it is: pure gift. There is nothing that we have not received. Yet thanksgiving from the heart is amazingly uncommon. The guest is confronted with truth. He knows that all is gift and the many talents and treasures freely given have been squandered. The *marred* gifts characterize ingratitude as do the used ones. There are few sins that cannot be traced back to a lack of charity and gratitude.

Herbert's psychological and spiritual acumen becomes evident in his dealing with the causal relationship between lust and blindness. The references in this short poem to seeing are numerous: 1) I cannot *look* on thee, 2) who made the *eye* but I, 3) *quick-eyed* love, 4) marred *vision*. Lust causes blindness; purity and love, vision. The sensual man lacks vision. St. John of the Cross writes:

> The appetite blinds and darkens the soul because the appetite as such is blind. It is blind because of itself it has no intellect. Reason always acts as a blind man's guide for the appetite. Consequently, every time a man's appetite leads him, he is blinded, just as we might say that when a blind man guides someone who has good eyesight both are blind.[5]

Lust, human sexuality run riot, is radically inhuman; it blocks the proper functioning of a person's spiritual, intellectual and even physical vision. One's humanity is lost in such a condition. The unchaste person, lacking insight and knowledge, flounders in a blinded decision-making process and is devoid of vital faith. As already noted, lust is grounded in a lack of charity ("unkind"), thus making more obvious the intimate connection between the gift of God's love received and the ability to perceive reality for what it truly is.

The hesitancy of the guest is grounded in no small matter. Love, the source of all light and goodness, the host with so much warmth and graciousness, encounters a scarred, self-accused sinner. Love encounters everyman! Herbert's experience resembles that of the psalmist: "Yahweh, who has the right to enter your tent, or to live on your holy mountain?" (15:1) Hesitancy characterizes the reverence with which a person approaches the invitation of the Divine Host. Who of us would or should respond differently?

The Banquet

Of sacred moments and sacred places there are few more important than the table. It is there that we welcome our nearest and dearest. To sit at table with someone is symbolic of a deeper reality: a oneness of mind and heart, a desired oneness of life. How painful it is to dine with people who have no shared values and experiences and affections. In his novel *Babbitt*, Sinclair Lewis gives a classic example of this awkwardness: "But he could not stir them. It was a dinner without a soul. For no reason that was clear to Babbitt, heaviness was over them and they spoke laboriously and unwillingly."[6]

In the God-human relationship, the place of communion often centers on the table, the sacrificial altar. In the breaking of bread and the sharing of the cup we ritualize the covenant reality. The Eucharist becomes the very center of revelation: the visibility of God's love in Jesus takes the form of the elements of the table. The sacred meal never allows us to forget the precious mystery of God's nearness and his desire to share himself with us. The hesitancy caused by a sense of unworthiness is in keeping with St. Paul's warning that we must not approach the table lightly. Herbert was conscious of this Pauline admonition.

The poet articulates well what religious experience means: a sitting down and a tasting of the reality of Love. Sitting down places a person in a passive, vulnerable position; it indicates a basic trust; it positions one in a dialogical situation. No longer self-motored (self-motivated), one becomes open to the other and is challenged to center outside of one's own self. This command, *sit down and eat*, is God's call to prayer. In this quiet time and gentle solitude, the art of love is experienced at the divine banquet. The truth is tasted; facts are encountered. The vital truth that God made the eye and by implication, all creation; the truth that he bore the blame and by implication, won reconciliation, is an objective fact. In entering the Lord's dwelling we begin to see. For the first time we experience the light and goodness of God, the very purpose of life. Resting in truth, goodness and beauty, the prayerful person is fulfilled and made whole. At the sacred table we are enriched, encouraged and renewed.

This is the meat, the truth. Milk can no longer satisfy. No *thing* can placate our appetite, only the living and true God. The solid stuff of life is the closeness of God, and being close to the source means being close to all creation with an accompanying love. As the Old Testament joyfully sings, "For what great nation is there that has gods so close to it as the Lord, our God, is to us whenever we call upon him?" (Deut 4:7) This is the truth that frees; this is the truth that gives meaning to life; this is the truth that reveals our true identity. Not to sit at table and taste the meat means not to experience life. It is to have "lived" without coming into contact with the fulness of reality. Life will have passed us by unless the invitation of the Divine Host is accepted. Then, of course, after the banquet has been tasted and savored, the service the poet promised will await doing.

1. Simone Weil, *Waiting for God*, trans. Emma Craufurd (New York: Harper Colophon Books, 1951) 68–69.

2. G. K. Chesterton, *The Everlasting Man* (New York: Doubleday & Company, Inc., 1955) 88.

3. C. S. Lewis, *Surprised by Joy: The Shape of My Early Life* (New York: Harcourt, Brace & World, Inc., 1955) 21.

4. Thomas Merton, *The Seven Storey Mountain* (New York: Harcourt Brace Jovanovich, Inc., 1948) 163.

5. *The Collected Works of St. John of the Cross*, trans. Kieran Kavanaugh, O.C.D., and Otilio Rodríguez, O.C.D. (ICS Publications, Institute of Carmelite Studies, Washington, 1973) 89–90.

6. Sinclair Lewis, *Babbitt* (New York: Harcourt Brace Jovanovich, Inc., 1922) 161.

5

Presence and a Psalm
Psalm 100: A Mini-Theology

Each of us lives a life gently shaped by the leading ideas that mold our minds, the profound affections that stir our hearts, and the meaningful relationships that give us a sense of identity. For believers, a primary source of influence is God's word. Through revelation we come to a realization of who we are and what we are about. Every so often there are passages of Scripture that magnificently summarize the core of our beliefs or highlight certain special moments of the relationship between God and humans. God's profound love for humans in Isa 43:1-5, the theme of covenant in Jer 31:31-34, the nearness of Yahweh in Hos 11:1-4, and God's plan of salvation shared by Paul in Eph 1:3-14 are just a few selections that could absorb our thoughts and hearts for many hours. In these brief passages the faith vision of God's people radiates with a special splendor and tends to unify our lives in the mystery of God's love and his tender forgiveness.

Besides the above mentioned texts, Psalm 100 might also serve as a concise mini-theology course: it is rich in truths, filled with the Spirit, and presents a faith vision that is sustaining and nourishing to the spiritual life. This chapter is an attempt to explicate the richness of this poetic prayer. Each person, however, must pass through the adit of the spiritual mine presented here and make the deeper journey individually.

A Psalm of Joy and Service

> Sing joyfully to the Lord, all you lands;
> serve the Lord with gladness;
> come before him with joyful song.

The immediate focus of this prayer is on the Lord. It is to him that we are urged to direct our song and hymn of praise; it is to the Lord and no other that we are to come. In popular parlance, he is number one. The centrality of the psalm is in direct opposition to the mystery of sinfulness in human life which puts self at the center of the stage. There is an innate tendency deeply rooted in our nature to sing to and of ourselves. As Walter Kerr writes in *The Decline of Pleasure*, "From the cut of our clothes to the slant of our souls we are sitting to have our portraits done." Would that egotistical singing were restricted to the shower room! It would be, if we adhered to the admonition of the psalmist, who directs our attention to God. The thrust is on the awareness of being truly present to the Lord. As the flight of an arrow takes its whole direction from its start, so too for prayer: the beginning is crucial. Centering on the Lord prevents us from getting lost in the song and in the singer. Otherwise the means become the end, the thing replaces the person, and prayer results in method rather than in personal relationship.

What is unobservable is hard to discern. The spirit of color underlying this hymn of praise is something that one must sense: sing *joyfully*, serve *with gladness*, come with *joyful* song. Not only is the content of prayer significant, but the manner or mode of disposition is also vital. Here we can speak of the quality or tone of prayer. In this psalm the tone is that of deep joy, a joy that flows from understanding that we are near to Truth and Goodness. Being possessed by a loving God should fill our whole person with joy and gladness. Even the many sorrows and sufferings of life are not incompatible with this basic disposition. In deep faith, these apparently negative experiences can be embraced in the knowledge that even hard moments can lead to happiness.

There are basically two ways of doing dishes, piling wood, doing one's homework: willingly or grudgingly. With the latter disposition a job can still be done efficiently (the dishes are clean, the wood is neatly piled, the assignments are completed), but the way in which they are accomplished destroys something in the doer and is certainly uncomfortable for anyone else in the near vicinity. The thesis that the way in which things are done is as important as what is done has a grain of truth. The psalmist is very insistent that the disposition of our prayer be that of joy and gladness. How tragic to come before the Lord grudgingly and unwillingly: do I have to pray, worship, go to church? By contrast, what greater joy is possible than for a person of faith to be with the Lord.

Perhaps our joy is somewhat muted. There abides within us the realization of having failed to respond to the generosity of the Father. This is cause for valid sadness in life. Further, because of our personal and collective sin, we are rightly embarrassed to face the gaze of the Holy One whom we have rejected or ignored in various ways. Heaviness of heart results from discouragement over weaknesses deeply engrained in our lives. Yet, edged with sorrow as the Christian life is, joy is the predominant mode of Christian existence because we focus more on God than on our own failings and selfishness. Just as Christian death must always be viewed in the light of the resurrection, so sin loses its ultimate sting in the perspective of a forgiving and loving Father. This muted joy concedes to the fact that the battle of life is still being waged and that we are in the process of being saved. It is not yet an accomplished fact in our personal existence, though victory is assured for those who accept the life of God and act in accord with it.

Besides the focus on God and the tonality of joy, the first three verses of our psalm are very dynamic in character. There is a challenge and an invitation to action: to sing, to serve, to come. Reflecting on the marvels of God—the beauty of creation, the key moments in salvation history, our personal blessings—our thoughts and affections cannot be contained by just a spoken word. Truly deep experiences demand dancing and skipping words in attempting to capture the depth of the encounter. Song becomes a sacred event when springing from a blessed or healed heart. Song basically is a response to some facet of God's goodness: songs of thanksgiving for blessing, songs of sorrow for our sins, songs of praise at catching a glimpse of God's glory.

The challenge to come before the Lord can be overwhelming. We fear the light for what it might reveal. The tendency to escape "down the nights and down the days" and to avoid the presence of God is understandable. Yet we cannot afford to run away from salvation, from love and forgiveness. Assuming full responsibility, we must respond to this invitation to come before the Lord as we are, with all the plus and minus aspects of our lives. We must make value judgments as to what we shall do with our limited time and energy. With the precious gift of freedom we can opt either for coming or going. Hopefully, graced with wisdom and confidence, we joyfully join the procession to the Lord in deep reverence. To come to the Lord goes beyond mere duty—it is an incredible privilege.

We are also invited and challenged to serve. No gasoline chain has the prerogative of saying, "Service is our business." This motto is at the heart of Christianity. Christ came to serve and not to be served. The root commandment is love and we cannot pass by our neighbor and still maintain that we love God. These two forms of love, though distinct, are inseparable. The basic elements of service and love are few: a willing heart, the ability to perceive the true needs of others, the development of necessary skills to meet these needs. The field of service is vast, ranging from spiritual direction to feeding the hungry of body. We serve by being for others in sharing what we have received. We serve by being present at moments of sorrow when nothing can be done except a touch on the shoulder or a compassionate gaze; we serve by rejoicing in the baseball victory of a small child; we serve by being receptive to the gifts that others must offer if they are to have a sense of importance. The spirit behind this service is gladness; we must be honored to be able to help. Christ has given us *the* example of serving, even unto death.

A Psalm of the Knowledge of God

> Know that the Lord is God;
> he made us, his we are;
> his people, the flock he tends.

Doubt and skepticism are constant companions of twentieth-century men and women. In an attempt to deal with the "big questions" of life there arises a sense of insecurity and frustration. In *The Shaping of Modern Thought*, Crane Brinton lists some of these questions:

> . . . cosmological questions, which ask whether the universe makes sense in terms of human capacity to comprehend and, if so, what kind of sense; theological and metaphysical questions, which ask further questions about purpose and design of the universe, and about man's place in it; and ethical and aesthetic questions, which ask whether what we do and what we want to do make sense, ask what we *really* mean by good and bad, by beautiful and ugly.

The volume of uncertainty is momentous in regard to such inquiries. Even though our bookstores flourish and educational institutions continue to multiply, human ignorance and the limitations of reasons are daily felt. The lyrics of our songs mirror what transpires in the human spirit: "What's it all about, Alfie?" (*Alfie*); "I really don't know clouds-life-love" (*Both Sides Now*); "Who can explain it, who can tell you why; fools give you reasons, wise men never try" (*Some Enchanted Evening*).

The psalmist, in profound and bold faith, speaks with conviction and encouraging certitude: "*Know* that the Lord is God." Here is fact; here is truth! Let doubt vanish, and let conviction and action step forward. In saying that the Lord is God the psalmist attempts to clarify a number of things. We are not masters of life and death. It is God who governs and "lords" us, in surprising gentleness and apparent powerlessness. The implication is obvious: before such a God we are servants, we are co-workers for the kingdom, we are friends, friends of the Lord! So often we have to be reminded that power, property, knowledge, food, fame, glory and even freedom (the boldest of all idols) are not God. These gifts are not to govern our lives but are to be used or discarded as they lead us to or take us away from the giver. The twentieth century has not yet discovered an immunity from idolatry; we are as susceptible to it as were people in any other period of history.

"He made us!" William Blake's poetry for children drives this truth home:

> Little Lamb, who made thee?
> Dost thou know who made thee?
> Gave thee life, and bade thee feed,
> By the stream and o'er the mead;
> Gave thee clothing of delight,
> Softest clothing, woolly, bright;
> Gave thee such a tender voice,
> Making all the vales rejoice?
> Little Lamb, who made thee?
> Dost thou know who made thee?
>
> Little Lamb, I'll tell thee,
> Little Lamb, I'll tell thee:
> He is called by thy name,
> For he calls Himself a lamb,
> He is meek, and He is mild;
> He became a little child.
> I a child, and thou a lamb,
> We are called by His name.
> Little Lamb, God bless thee!
> Little Lamb, God bless thee!

As Blake questions the animal world, and implicitly all of life, we sense a profound and ultimate truth: "All life, all holiness comes from God" (Eucharistic Prayer III). God is the root and ground of all being; he is the source and principle of all creation. The implication for us is the mystery of creatureliness. To be made, to be created means to be both totally dependent and totally gifted, totally contingent and totally real. This truth sheds some light on the healthy feeling of poverty arising within human consciousness at strange moments of existence.

The deist acknowledges God but from a distance. God does exist, but once having begun the process of life, is now no longer radically involved or concerned with the plight of man. This psalm argues to the contrary. There is a special and intimate bond that exists between the Creator and his creature. It is as if God has posted "wanted" signs throughout the universe, for we are his people and he carefully tends our life down to the numbering of the hairs on our heads. The need to belong and to be wanted by another is fulfilled in this relationship. God claims us as his own. We are his special possession. From this perspective a more radical question than who we are is the question whose we are: who or what really possesses us? It is in this relational question that we begin to discover our true identity. Self-knowledge is now in direct proportion to our knowledge of God. The plea of the psalmist becomes very urgent: know, please know *this* God. Truth leads to freedom; to be embraced by this loving Father is to move into the land of freedom.

To be tended is not the prerogative of babies and gardens. All creation needs to be tended, cared for, loved. Our God does not make us and then ignore us. The affectionate concern of God for His people is clear in the writings of Hosea:

> I myself taught Ephraim to walk,
> I took them in my arms;
> yet they have not understood that I was the one looking after them.
> I led them with reins of kindness,
> with leading-strings of love.
> I was like someone who lifts an infant close against his cheek;
> stooping down to him I gave him his food (11:3-4).

Having to choose between being murdered or being consistently ignored, someone once facetiously selected the former. Underlying the choice was the truth that not to be in meaningful relationships with life-supporting people is already to live in hell. Our God not only does not ignore us, he is a TLC God (a God of *tender, loving care*). Growth and happiness are fostered in this experiential knowledge. St. Paul came to know this type of God in the risen Christ. And far from living a Pollyanna existence, Paul often testified to the suffering and pain that were essential ingredients in his religious life. Even these moments were subtle forms of God's tenderness showing itself in mysterious ways. Basically, the psalmist is convinced that the tenderness and intimacy of God pervade the entire life of the faith person.

Ignorance is usually a great tragedy. This psalm is an urgent plea that we become aware and retain an abiding consciousness of the *fact* that God is our Lord, he made us, we are indeed his special possession and that, as his people, we are lovingly cared for. Were this truth to truly penetrate our hearts, a transformation would necessarily take place. Left in the abstract, it sounds vaguely nice but quickly evaporates like the morning dew. In the concrete, this prayer challenges us to do the truth and comforts us in inviting us to rest in the source of the truth, the Lord.

A Psalm of Praise and Thanksgiving

> Enter his gates with thanksgiving,
> his courts with praise;
> Give thanks to him; bless his name.

Sensing the strong and constant desire of God to possess us as his people, the psalmist now urges us to enter into God's presence. Using the images of gates and courts, he invites us to come before the Lord. But this is an invitation; each of us has the capacity either to enter in or to remain separated from divine intimacy. To pass through these gates is to leave behind the immediacy of other experiences, though we cannot leave behind what has formed and shaped our existence. We bring our whole self through these gates which lead to a deeper and more explicit awareness of our God. Just as we can remain outside ourselves, so too we can remain outside the nearness of the Lord. Teresa of Avila's reflection speaks of a recurring problem: "There are souls so infirm and so accustomed to busying themselves with outside affairs that nothing can be done for them, and it seems as though they are incapable of entering within themselves at all." To enter into the presence of another person, one must be willing to let go, to surrender oneself to the present moment. Gates imply both a passage and at times an obstacle. A journey must be made if there is to be presence, but the journey and entrance can be accomplished only if the gates are known. Again Teresa uses the image of a gate: "Prayer and reflection are the gateway into his Castle."

A second image used to stress oneness with the Lord is entrance into his courts. Unfamiliar as we are in our times with such regal terms, there is no difficulty in sensing the majesty and awesomeness of this scene. A human person now stands before the Creator. Though the courts are filled with the companions of God, the saints from all the ages, the focus is on the King as ruler and governor of all things. A court is a dwelling, though here non-geographical. Wherever God is, there is his court and his power and his gentleness. We are invited into this kingdom; we are invited to breathe its atmosphere and to taste its joys.

There are two responses urged upon us as we come before our God: thanksgiving and praise. To give thanks was a common activity in the life of Christ. He gave us an example and has called us to be Eucharistic people. Sensing that all is gift and grace, we naturally respond with thanksgiving. Children have to be asked what they should say upon receiving some present; mature adults do not have to be asked since they respond spontaneously with heartfelt gratitude. With faith there is a constant readiness to attribute to God every blessing of life. Without faith, most things are taken for granted and grace fails to find a receptive home.

A more profound response is that of praise. Whereas the giver of thanks has a propensity to center on the gift, the person of praise must necessarily center on the person being praised. Romano Guardini reflects on the notion of praise (adoration) as he speaks about humankind's worship of God:

> "We thank Thee for Thy great glory." What does that mean? Do we not thank a person for what he gives, rather than for what he is? But the words express the thought exactly. That God exists and that He is what He is constitutes no mere necessity, or fact, but a grace and a blessing. Yes, it is true, we are permitted to thank Him for His mere being. And here lies the root of adoration (praise). It is the bowing down of all creation before God, not only because He is all-powerful but because He is worthy as well.

The mystery here is overwhelming and challenging—overwhelming since we are called to a deep knowledge of God as he is in himself; challenging as well, in that we must abandon our preoccupations with self and things in order to be present totally to the other. Experiencing how difficult it is even to be present to each other, we should hardly be surprised that we must struggle to surrender our selfishness to the triune God.

Unlike the rest of creation, which is unable to articulate gratitude and praise, the human person has these capacities. Proper recognition and acknowledgement become possible for sensitive human beings. The attitudes and actions of thankfulness and praise express the rich potential of human life; absence of these tells of humankind's deepest sins. Shakespeare's insight rings true: "How sharper than a serpent's tooth it is to have a thankless child." Ingratitude denies the religious nature of humans and turns life into a lie. Taking things for granted (a more subtle, though no less devastating form of ingratitude) leads to insensitivity and a breakdown of what was once a personal relationship. Not to praise is not to see. Spiritual cataracts can develop within anyone's life. The blindness that results from jealousy, fear and envy obstructs the recognition of the values in others as well as God. If, in our human relationships, it is difficult to admit the worth of others for various reasons, how much more trouble we will have in accepting the supremacy of the Lord. Thomas More writes in his *Utopia* of the hostile movements of the heart: "Now if in such a Court, made up of persons who envy all others and only admire themselves, a person should but propose anything that he had either read in history, or observed in his travel, the rest would think that the reputation of their wisdom would sink." Even with God we incredibly vie for ascendancy, worried that if he is praised we are the less for it. We cannot successfully compete with God; sanity demands that God be praised by his creatures. Any other path is doomed to lead nowhere but to darkness and death.

Many saints are exemplars in their praise and thanksgiving. St. Augustine was one who entered God's courts with thanksgiving and deep praise; for that reason he now shares in the fulness of God's life. In his writing Augustine shares with us his response to God's goodness.

> But yet, Lord, thanks must be given to you, our God, the most excellent and best creator and ruler of the universe, even if you had willed only to bring me to childhood. Even then I existed, had life and feeling, had care for my own well-being, which is a trace of your own most mysterious unity from which I took my being. By my inner sense I guarded the integrity of my outer senses, and I delighted in truth, in these little things and in thoughts about these little things. I did not want to err; I was endowed with a strong memory; I was well instructed in speech; I was refined by friendship, I shunned sadness, dejection and ignorance. What was there that was not wonderful and praiseworthy in such a living being?

All these things are the gifts of my God; I did not give them to myself (*Confessions*, bk. 1, ch. 20).

A Psalm of God's Goodness, Kindness and Faithfulness

Indeed, how good is the Lord
whose kindness endures forever,
and his faithfulness to all generations.

Ideas mold lives. Our working concept of God has profound and lasting consequences on our everyday lives. A major distortion here leads to harmful behavioral patterns and possibly a meaningless existence. Walter Kerr's reflection that "an infection begun in the mind will reach every extremity" emphasizes the importance of a solid theological education. One does not have to travel far or talk at any great length to discover various destructive and inaccurate notions of God. A satellite god, distant, hidden behind cloud covers, is far removed from the human heart. Such an impersonal god elicits no expectant faith. Literature gives us hints of this notion of God: "The pastor of the First Christian Church of Monarch, a large man with a long damp frontal lock, informed God that the real estate men were here now" (Sinclair Lewis, *Babbitt*).

No more healthy is the Olympian god. For the Greeks, Mt. Olympus was filled with strange and wrathful deities who were not far enough away, who were too involved in the affairs of men and women. This is a god of fear, thunder and punishment. Perhaps even James and John, in asking Jesus to call down fire from heaven to destroy a Samaritan town for its lack of hospitality, had a highly distorted notion of the Father. At least Jesus reprimanded them for their suggestion and misguided enthusiasm. An Olympian god is irrational, whimsical and arbitrary. Lacking any degree of constancy, a person might have to approach this god as a schoolboy who on a spring day pulls petals from a daisy as he tries to figure out his relationship with a girl he is fond of: "She loves me, she loves me not." The God of Scripture does not cause such doubt for he is a God of fidelity, constancy, and unconditional love.

The psalmist presents God as a God of goodness, kindness and faithfulness. These are the reasons for the praise and thanksgiving called for earlier in the psalm. What is crucial here is experience. We must personally "taste and see the goodness of the Lord." This is available for those who have eyes to see God's goodness in the beauties and splendors of creation, in the stars and rivers, in the human face, in the person of Jesus. In the face of total goodness we confront mystery: a God without evil! Our minds falter before such a reality. We fall back on the experiences of goodness from our personal histories and magnify these to the *nth* degree, trying hopefully to catch a passing glimpse of this quality within our God. Our faith tells us that only if the Father reveals this mystery to us can we hope to see. St. Paul, who was open to such a gift, had his whole life reshaped when he experienced the goodness of the Lord. With deep conviction he writes to the Corinthians: ". . . if anyone is in Christ, he is a new creation. The old order has passed away; now all is new!" (2 Cor 5:17) The goodness of God is dynamic; it gives life. The psalmist himself was blessed to taste and see that God was good to him; he shares this experience with us and urges us to enter into the same reality. If we have consistently missed this experience, or have not leisure enough to enter into it, by singing this poetic song we are privileged to taste anew the mystery of God's working among us. "We who were denied the first experience or were not sufficiently idle to have it, are offered the pleasure of playing over his work until we find, unexpectedly, what he has found for us."[1]

People are radically vulnerable to kindness. Since God is kindness itself, anyone who comes to know the living and true God will be wounded by his love. Kindness, conceived by modern man, has some strange forms: we can kill with kindness, we can allow a softness to replace a healthy notion of gentle strength, we can divorce kindness from sacrifice. God's kindness is mixed with love and is not a stranger to suffering. In fact, kindness which automatically excludes suffering is to be severely questioned. C. S. Lewis succinctly captures the relationship between love-kindness and suffering:

> It is for people whom we care nothing about that we demand happiness on any terms: with our friends, our lovers, our children, we are exacting and would rather see them suffer much than be happy in contemptible and estranging modes. If God is Love, He is, by definition, something more than mere kindness. And it appears, from all the records, that though He has often rebuked us and condemned us, He has never regarded us with contempt. He has paid us the intolerable compliment of loving us, in the deepest, most tragic, most inexorable sense.[2]

God desires our happiness. If suffering is necessary for this goal to be achieved, his kindness will include it. However, there is a danger that the presence of suffering fosters a hostile notion of God: a God of meanness, a God who holds grudges. Such notions are totally erroneous if we truly comprehend the real meaning of kindness which the psalmist shares with us.

Though generations "have trod, have trod, have trod," our God remains eternally faithful. The fickleness of March, the impermanency of a flower, the termination of an engagement are accurate analogies to use in describing the movements of the human heart; not so with God. His love is constant and faithful. Our personalities are often fickle (and sometimes freckled), our hearts are nomadic—dashing quickly down many false avenues, our identity is much more glacial than we suppose. Our response to God's love is terribly contingent; his fidelity is awesomely necessary!

The most obvious proof of fidelity is presence. Faith is of major importance here: that we truly believe in God's nearness in his word, in the sacrament, in the face of a fellow pilgrim, in all creation. Even in the darkest moments of human experience, right in the center of death and sin, God is available to us for the asking. A horrid temptation is to misconceive our God: God has left us to ourselves, life is meaningless, there are no ultimate answers. Skepticism begins its hellish growth; confidence gives way to doubt; courage yields to fear. The categorical imperative of life is to get in touch with the truth: the truth is that God forever manifests his love in his goodness, kindness and fidelity.

Psalm 100 Paraphrased

"Come, my friends, come people of every land and nation, and with a song of profound joy let us together sing to our Lord who stands before us. Let us not only sing with joy but let our hands and lives truly serve our God with a glad spirit. With reverence let us be with him and hymn a cheerful tone.

We must never forget that the Lord is our God, our beloved. We must always remember that he made and makes us ever new. We must realize at every moment that we belong to him, that we are his family, that he carefully tends us as does a shepherd his flock.

For these many reasons we must travel through the gates of his home, come into the room where he dwells. There we shall say thank you and in deep awe praise our King. May his name and person be blessed always.

We must comprehend these facts: our Lord is good, he is always kind in his love, he never leaves us to ourselves. Indeed, 'no wonder of it,' that we must sing, thank, praise and bless so gracious a God."

1. Walter Kerr, *The Decline of Pleasure* (New York: Simon & Schuster, Inc., 1962) 192.

2. C. S. Lewis, *The Problem of Pain* (New York: Macmillan Publishing Co., Inc., 1962) 41.

6

Presence and Principles
Principles of Prayer

Growth in all forms of relationships, be they with God or with one another, calls for an ongoing communication process. Prayer is one such process involving dialogue between God and the human person. In order to be meaningful that process must be grounded on certain principles descriptive of universal conditions, consequences and causes of meaningful prayer.

This chapter culls out ten principles of prayer as articulated by various spiritual authors. These authors, experiencing prayer at different levels according to the uniqueness of their personality structures, share in written form some truths that provide an explication of prayer experiences in general. These truths when understood in context may well enlighten our own experiences or at least cause us to desire them as we journey to the Father. In so doing we can grow in our dialogical relationship with God.

A three-step method will be used: 1) a statement of a principle of prayer; 2) a series of quotations from which the principle was drawn, or of quotations used to demonstrate the validity of the principle; and 3) a commentary developing some implications buried within the principle and/or quotations.

Though principles are significant and advantageous in providing a perspective and pointing out a direction, experience itself is the central concern. Hopefully, as the reader journeys beyond the principle into the experience that it elucidates, he or she will find deeper meaning in it and be able to come into contact with the principal Reality underlying all real principles.

1. Prayer is essentially loving attention.[1]

> Thus the individual also should proceed only with a loving attention to God, without making specific acts. He should conduct himself passively, as we have said, without efforts of his own, but with the simple, loving awareness, as a person who opens his eyes with loving attention.[2]
>
> Attention animated by desire is the whole foundation of religious practices.[3]
>
> I shall not dwell upon this because I want to say something about the way in which I think those of us who practice prayer may profit, though everything is profitable to a soul that loves the Lord with fervent desire, since it instills into it courage and wonder.[4]

Two essential elements of authentic prayer are contained in the definition of prayer as loving attention: awareness of the presence of the Other and a heartfelt, concerned response. Distraction within consciousness and indifference of the heart block meaningful communication with God. If, on our part, we are called to love with attention, this is consequent upon God's loving attention toward us. God made us; he is attentive to the smallest detail of our lives; he loves us completely. An affirmative answer must be given to Blake's deeply religious question: "Did he smile his work to see?"

The Father's loving attention has been revealed in Jesus, the Word incarnate. A coming-to-visit verifies God's love and awareness. Further verification is found in the sending of the Spirit into our lives, the Spirit of love and knowledge. Because of this personal Grace we are enabled to truly pray:

> The Spirit too comes to help us in our weakness. For when we cannot choose words in order to pray properly, the Spirit himself expresses our plea in a way that could never be put into words, and God who knows everything in our hearts knows perfectly well what he means, and that the pleas of the saints expressed by the Spirit are according to the mind of God.[5]

Defining prayer in terms of loving attention is simple but not simplistic. Its simplicity lies in its directness and succinctness; it is not reductionistic, because neither love nor attentiveness is easily attained. Prayer, like all great acts, defies full analysis because it contains too much mystery. Only knowledge of prayer from the inside, that is, through experience, allows for even surface knowledge of such a powerful event.

2. Prayer is proportionate to the quality of one's love.[6]

> Farewell, farewell! but this I tell
> To thee, thou Wedding-Guest!
> He prayeth well, who loveth well
> Both man and bird and beast.
>
> He prayeth best, who loveth best
> All things both great and small;
> For the dear God who loveth us,
> He made and loveth all.[7]

> [St. Francis] knew that without prayer true love was impossible, and he learned from living that without love prayer became self-centered and barren.[8]

> I repeat that if you have this in view you must not build upon foundations of prayer and contemplation alone, for, unless you strive after the virtues and practice them, you will never grow to be more than dwarfs. God grant that nothing worse than this may happen—for, as you know, anyone who fails to go forward begins to go back, and love, I believe, can never be content to stay for long where it is.[9]

The spiritual life demands balance. How one relates to God in prayer is intimately related to how one encounters his neighbor. Scripture is transparent on this point: one who says that he or she loves God and at the same time shows hatred to his or her neighbor is a liar.[10] The person who spends an hour in prayer while neglecting the obvious needs of people close at hand must seriously examine the authenticity of such prayer. Indeed, the touchstone for one's prayer life is fraternal charity.[11]

Prayer and love are symbiotic. Since our God is Love, we must be in close contact with him if we are to share that gift with others to its fullest. The reverse is also true: unless we share the love given in prayer, the gift dries up or simply engenders pride. As in all provinces of life, the principle of interdependence applies directly to the spiritual life, too. Integration of prayer and love, contemplation and virtue, liturgy and the apostolate are called for. Isolation and fragmentation here create a false spirituality visible to everyone except their possessor. A vision of integrated spirituality and a discipline of courageous action is true imitation of Christ.

3. Genuine prayer demands some self-control of body and spirit.[12]

> . . . we shall not fail to observe the fasts, disciplines and periods of silence which the order commands; for, as you know, if prayer is to

be genuine it must be reinforced with these things—prayer cannot be accompanied by self-indulgence.[13]

Oh, who can tell how impossible it is for a man with appetites to judge the things of God as they are?[14]

We shall have overcome a considerable obstacle when prayer and penance condition each other, for their unity will be able to become the guarantee of their orientation. If it is necessary to deprive oneself of food and sleep, it is not to establish a performance or glorify oneself over an exploit, but to allow the spirit to give itself freely to prayer, since, if it is less strongly captivated by the things of earth, it will be able to give attention to what is above it.[15]

When the body or the spirit is not free but addicted to various substances or objects, the process of prayer is threatened. A body satiated with food and drink becomes listless and weary; a mind constantly filled with the flood of stimuli is so preoccupied as not to be receptive to other realities. Prayer is premised upon the ability to say no to one level of reality so as to be able to say yes to the workings of the Holy Spirit.

Asceticism is a condition that creates space and time for dialogue with God. Certain exercises, such as fasting, periods of extended silence, or voluntary mortification, are means by which that space and time become real. The "if-then principle" applies to spirituality as it does to all of life: if farmers want the fall harvest, then they must willingly do the spring plowing and planting; if people want to listen and respond to the Lord, then the time and space must be created for the encounter to happen. Strong and determined desire lies at the root of such discipline.

Self-control extends one step beyond asceticism. Once the emptiness has been created through exercises done out of love, the soul must wait on the Lord, who will come in his own time and in his own manner. Waiting for God is at the heart of prayer and is already a deep form of prayer; self-control makes that waiting possible, and grace makes it sacred. Although not speaking of prayer, C. S. Lewis describes well an aspect of the human condition: "Then came the worst part, the waiting."[16]

4. In prayer, I must bring this me to the living and true God.[17]

I enter into the presence of God with all my load of misery and troubles. And he takes me as I am and makes me to be alone with Him.[18]

> If you're approaching Him not as the goal but as a road, not as the end but as a means, you're not really approaching Him at all.[19]
>
> I can testify that this is one of the most grievous kinds of life which I think can be imagined, for I had neither any joy in God nor any pleasure in the world. When I was in the midst of wordly pleasures, I was distressed by the remembrance of what I owed to God; when I was with God, I grew restless because of worldly affections.[20]

Any genuine conversation requires that each participant have an adequate level of self-knowledge and be familiar with the content under discussion. Where either is wanting, communication breaks down. Prayer, which is essentially a form of communication, requires the same: we must know our real self and have some notion of who God is as well as understand the experience being shared. Because we always want to come off looking good, it is difficult to bring our real, true self to God without editing. Because God can be conceived in ways that are distortions of his true nature, it can easily happen that we attempt to pray to gods that do not exist. One of the greatest causes of sterility in prayer is a misconception of God and a failure to be in touch with our true identity.

Psychologists are helpful in depicting for us a variety of selves with which we must deal:

> Each of us seems to have three *self-concepts*. The *personal* self-image is how the individual pictures his most inner self ("how I really am"). The *social* self is how he thinks others see him, and the pattern of responses he learns in order to be a social being. The *ideal* self is made up of the goals set by parents, the culture, and other sources ("how I *should* be"). Often, these three conflict, creating problems for the individual trying to satisfy them all.[21]

Each person must examine which of these selves is operative not only in the interactions of one's daily life but also as one comes before God. To play a role in the presence of the Lord prohibits encounter with our deepest self. To demand that our ideal self (perfectionism) be actualized before we pray only leads to a guilt trip. God says to us, "Come as you are—no need for formal dress here."

C. S. Lewis knew that God cannot be captured by our finite reason: "My idea of God is not a divine idea. It has to be shattered time after time."[22] Yet we can come to some knowledge of the living and true God. As Christians we attain to this through faith and knowledge of Jesus Christ. In Jesus, our God is made visible. Gifted with the Spirit, we make our journey to the Father in and through Jesus. His life, death, and resurrection are a summary statement of the Father's love and forgiveness. Thus all of our prayer passes through, and is enriched by, Jesus as we speak to and listen to the Father.

Authentic prayer demands authentic persons. Our real self must be continually searched out; our real God must be longed for and awaited in silence and solitude. Only when real people meet can dialogue take place. The dialogue of prayer is no exception.

5. Prayer's primary focus is on God, not on self or on events.[23]

> I get nowhere by looking at myself; I merely get discouraged. So I am making the resolution to abandon myself entirely to God, to look only at him, to leave all the care of myself to him, to practice only one thing, *confidence;* my extreme wretchedness, my natural cowardice leaving me no other way to go to God and to advance in good.[24]

> It is not my business to think about myself. My business is to think about God. It is for God to think about me.[25]

> You could, if you wished, deny that Mister God existed, but then any denial didn't alter the fact that Mister God was. No, Mister God was, he *was* the kingpin, the center, the very heart of things; and this is where it got funny. You see, we had to recognize that he was all these things, and that meant that we were at our center, not God. God is our center, and yet it is we who acknowledge that he is the center. That makes us somehow internal to Mister God. This is the curious nature of Mister God: that even while he is at the center of all things, he waits outside us and knocks to come in. It is we who open the door. Mister God doesn't break it down and come in; no, he knocks and waits.[26]

Focusing and centering are concepts and experiences that are emphasized in spirituality and psychology. Through this activity we realize that what is at the core of our consciousness radically affects our thoughts, feelings, and actions. Often a violent struggle takes place in the deepest part of our being as various persons, forces, and things vie for centrality.

Prayer deals directly with centering. Our experience indicates how easily self-centeredness moves in or how daily anxieties and worries can become so strong as to exclude any awareness of a loving, caring God. Self-transcendence is no easy task; trust that the Lord will provide is more easily thought than experienced. Only in grace can the obstacles blocking our encounter with God be removed. Jesus' prayer and life were centered on the Father and the doing of his will.

Often in the early hours and before major events, Jesus explicitly turned to the Father in deep, familiar communication. These explicit moments were indications of an implicit, hidden life of union. How else explain the intimacy of the Last Supper discourse? Yet Jesus, in his humanness, must have struggled at times to keep proper focus. We need but ponder his agony in the garden to realize that the struggle we have with ourselves and our fear of suffering were part of Jesus' experience as well.

The lives of the saints are records of people who struggled to center on God in spite of their own selfishness. Augustine's ongoing conversion, Teresa of Avila's admission that for years her prayer was superficial, John of the Cross' constant challenge to mortification lest the self dominate—all manifest the eternal conflict between the ego and divine love. Marvelously God withholds rest so that we can never be fully at peace unless we center on him. George Herbert saw this and recorded it magnificently:

> When God at first made man,
> Having a glass of blessings standing by,
> Let us (said he) pour on him all we can;
> Let the world's riches, which dispersed lie,
>   Contract into a span.
>
> So strength first made a way;
> Then beauty flow'd, then wisdom, honour, pleasure:
> When almost all was out, God made a stay,
> Perceiving that, alone of all his treasure,
>   Rest in the bottom lay.
>
> For if I should (said he)
> Bestow this jewel also on my creature,
> He would adore my gifts instead of me,
> And rest in Nature, not the God of Nature:
>   So both should losers be.
>
> Yet let him keep the rest,
> But keep them with repining restlessness;
> Let him be rich and weary, that at least,
> If goodness lead him not, yet weariness
>   May toss him to my breast.[27]

6. Silence, solitude, and surrender are conditions for prayer.[28]

> When it happens, therefore, that a person is conscious in this manner of being placed in solitude and in the state of listening, he should

> even forget the practice of loving attentiveness I mentioned so as to remain free for what the Lord then desires of him.[29]
>
> The beginning of integrity is not effort but surrender; it is simply the opening of the heart to receive that for which the heart is longing. The healing of mankind begins whenever any man ceases to resist the love of God.[30]
>
> Good as is discourse, silence is better, and shames it. The length of the discourse indicates the distance of thought betwixt the speaker and the hearer. If they were at a perfect understanding in any part, no words would be necessary thereon. If at one in all parts, no words would be suffered.[31]

This SSS principle (Silence, Solitude, Surrender) establishes the dispositions allowing for union with God. Simply by looking at their opposites we realize how important they are. Constant chatter impedes prayer ("In your prayers do not babble as the pagans do"—Matt 6:5); crowding our lives with activities and people stifles the inner agenda; clutching desperately to our own wills thwarts the realization of the Father's will.

In a culture that is activistic and grasping, silence, solitude, and surrender are not easy to come by. We must recognize the influence of the external environment on the internal milieu. Diligence and discipline are required if we are to grow in a rich, interior silence; courage and trust, if we are to dwell alone with the Other; love and generosity, if we are to accomplish the Lord's will freely.

The attainment of a given end necessitates appropriate means. The house of the Lord is attained by traveling the path of silence, solitude, and surrender. The path is narrow, perhaps peopled by few. Desire for union with God provides the enthusiasm to set out and continue on the journey. The greatest tragedy is to ignore the voices that call us to love, to dwell with many and not to have the One, to retain a false freedom at the cost of life.

7. The tone of prayer is one of reverence and awe.[32]

> Then prayer is a witness that the soul wills as God wills, and it eases the conscience and fits man for grace. And so he teaches us to pray and to have firm trust that we shall have it; for he beholds us in love, and wants to make us partners in his good will and work.[33]
>
>> Earth's crammed with heaven
>> And every common bush afire with God;
>> And only he who sees takes off his shoes—
>> The rest sit round and pluck blackberries.[34]

First, therefore, I invite the reader
to the groans of prayer
through Christ crucified,
through whose blood
we are cleansed from the filth of vice—
so that he not believe
that reading is sufficient without unction,
speculation without devotion,
investigation without wonder,
observation without joy,
work without piety,
knowledge without love,
understanding without humility,
endeavor without divine grace,
reflection as a mirror without divinely inspired wisdom.[35]

A personal attitude toward a particular person or object is known as tone. Hostility, lack of openness, and prejudices are negative attitudes creating an atmosphere (tone) of fear and discomfort; gentleness, respect, and affability are positive attitudes promoting a climate (tone) of warmth and joy. The interior manner by which we approach God is of great importance in prayer. Julian of Norwich writes that when one is comfortable in coming to the Lord, deeper experiences of prayer are possible: "And so prayer makes harmony between God and man's soul, because when man is at ease with God he does not need to pray, but to contemplate reverently what God says."[36]

Though our tone is important, of greater significance is the manner in which God comes to us in prayer. God's attitude flows from his nature, a nature that is summarized in the word "love." And love's cousins are reverence and awe. What mystery here—our God is so gracious and courteous in his visitations to us! Julian of Norwich shares her experience of God's tonality: "Of everything which I saw, this was the greatest comfort to me, that our Lord is so familiar and so courteous, and this most filled my soul with delight and surety."[37]

When we enter into prayer, it is of great profit to ask for the Spirit of reverence and awe, the same Spirit that empowered Jesus as he addressed the Father in silence and solitude. Reverence and awe are essentially gifts and are to be asked for. When we are gifted with these gentle attitudes, our prayer takes on an entirely different quality. Without these gifts our hearts are stifled and our service cool. The reverent feel deeply and serve generously; the awe-filled see with wonder and hear with trembling.

8. God's activity in prayer is far more important than our activity.[38]

Prayer is a personal response to God's presence. It is more something that God does to us, rather than anything we do. This means that God first makes Himself present to us. Prayer is our awareness of and then response to God.[39]

In this interior union God communicates Himself to the soul with such genuine love that no mother's affection, in which she tenderly caresses her child, nor brother's love, nor friendship is comparable to it. The tenderness and truth of love by which the immense Father favors and exalts this humble and loving soul reaches such a degree—O wonderful thing, worthy of all our awe and admiration—that the Father Himself becomes subject to her for her exaltation, as though he were her servant and she His lord. And He is as solicitous in favoring her as He would be if He were her slave and she His god. So profound is the humility and sweetness of God![40]

In the first place it should be known that if a person is seeking God, his Beloved is seeking him much more.[41]

Self-sufficiency is a trait much admired by our culture. Nothing happens unless we make it happen; being responsible implies the total management of our lives, including the spiritual domain. Control is the goal. With such a mentality, it is not surprising that God's invitations and graces fall on deaf ears and are unseen because of our blindness. We simply are not open to outside motivation; we are dancers who must always lead. The consequence of such a disposition is tragic: "A person extinguishes the spirit by wanting to conduct himself in a way different from that in which God is leading him."[42]

While acknowledging both the necessity and health of self-reliance in its deepest meaning, complete self-motivation leads to stagnation and death. Faith tells us that God always takes the initiative, that Christian life is a radical response to what God speaks and calls us to do. In no way does this deny the principle that we are challenged to make things happen, not just let them happen. But that making is consequent upon the word of our Father. The Christian heart, in wisdom, seeks simply to please the Father, whatever is asked. Though the request may be surrounded by darkness, though his thoughts and ways differ from our own, the challenge will remain the same: "Our task is always the humble and courageous one of listening obediently and acting boldly."[43] Our activity must flow from that deep listening to the word of God. The day should begin with a listening disposition; it should end with a review of our response to the Father's word.

Thus, prayer is dialogic: a word is spoken in love and answered out of love. The answer itself becomes the substance for the next movement in the warm, mutual relationship between God and his creature. The familiarity here is profound; its absence creates an incredible loneliness and a haunting restlessness.

9. There is no one way of praying; pluralism in prayer must be carefully safeguarded.[44]

> If while the soul is meditating the Lord should suspend it, well and good; for in that case He will make it cease meditation even against its own will. I consider it quite certain that this method of procedure is no hindrance to the soul but a great help to it in everything that is good; whereas, if it laboured hard at meditation in the way I have already described, this would indeed be a hindrance—in fact, I believe such labour is impossible for a person who has attained greater heights. This may not be so with everyone, since God leads souls by many ways, but those who are unable to take this road should not be condemned or judged incapable of enjoying the great blessings contained in the mysteries of Jesus Christ our God.[45]
>
> I do not say this without reason, for, as I have said, it is very important for us to realize that God does not lead us all by the same road, and perhaps she who believes herself to be going along the lowest road is the highest in the Lord's eyes. So it does not follow that, because all of us in this house practice prayer, we are all *perforce* to be contemplatives.[46]
>
> God leads each one along different paths so that hardly one spirit will be found like another in even half its method of procedure.[47]

Uniqueness of personality structure helps to specify what form and style of prayer are most appropriate for the individual. God works with and through our individuality. How dangerous, therefore, to simply adopt someone else's manner of praying. Sheer imitation is not only foolish but can be injurious to one's spiritual life, leading to frustration and discouragement. A popular expression states, "Different strokes for different folks!" So in the spiritual life: different prayers for different cares. Prayer is as varied as people, with the commonality coming in the word-response pattern underlying all communication between God and his people.

Just as prayer varies from person to person, it also varies within each person's life. During certain periods of faith development, vocal and formal prayer may well be the best form of prayer for that time; at other stages, meditative or contemplative prayer may be in order.

Further, prayer styles may change within the course of a single week, even in the course of a single hour. Form and style are not the heart of the matter; what is of essence is personal encounter with God. Once that experience happens, we simply rest in his presence. "As soon as God's word makes its impact, we must leave all the rest and follow it."[48] Prayer is a means to an end, and the end is union with God. The paths to union are multiple.

Pluralism is threatened by stereotyping and rigid conformity. Granting the validity, indeed the necessity, of a certain measure of uniformity in public prayer, the principle to be followed in personal, private prayer is that of freedom. Only the individual knows the context of his or her own life; it is this context that sets the parameters for the form and style of prayer. Because our context is continually changing, prayer forms must be adapted accordingly. Thus pluralism becomes a principle necessary for spiritual health and growth.

10. Prayer leads to intimacy with God and to solidarity with all creation.[49]

> It should be noted that until the soul reaches this state of union of love, she should practice love in both the active and contemplative life. Yet once she arrives, she should not become involved in other works and exterior exercises that might be of the slightest hindrance to the attentiveness of love toward God, even though the work be of great service to God. For a little of this pure love is more precious to God and the soul and more beneficial to the Church, even though it seems one is doing nothing, than all these other works put together.[50]

> In prayer I can enter into contact with the God who created me and all things out of love. In prayer I can find a new sense of belonging since it is there that I am most related.[51]

> We are put on earth a little space,
> That we may learn to bear the beams of love.[52]

Activities find their meaning in terms of their goal. The end of the spiritual life is union with God, and by means of this unity we are mysteriously united to all creation. Oneness is attained by love; prayer is a central love-act in our lives. Through ongoing communication with God, we grow in mutual knowledge and respect until one day we awake to an intimacy incapable of description. The bonding here is subtle and mysterious, powerful and challenging. The Lord stands at the door knocking, and a choice has to be made. Following our *Fiat*, God comes to dwell with us, and our homes are never the same.

Prayer's unifying power does not terminate in intimacy with God alone. Authentic prayer necessitates an ever deeper union with our brothers and sisters. To be united to the Father means to be united to his children, the entire family of God. The closer we are to the cross of Christ and the power of the Spirit, the closer we are to all of life. By touching the fountain of life and holiness, we touch all creation. Thus, without prayer a sense of alienation and isolation invades our hearts. Separated from the source, we cannot come into vital contact with the created world. Prayer gives us entrance not only into the heart of our triune God but also into the mystery of his loving creation.

Because prayer fosters intimacy, it is not uncommon for fear to block our communication with God. Intimacy means to know and to be known whole; such radical sharing implies the possibility of radical rejection. Perhaps we are not sure that we are all that lovable. Thus it is in faith and trust that we approach our God, believing that he loves us unconditionally; it is with humility and courage that we approach our brothers and sisters, knowing that through grace we can accept them and they can accept us. Prayer involves revelation, acceptance, and humility; it demands faith, trust, and courage. Gifted by the Spirit, we enter the land of prayer and therein find our happiness.

The Journey and the Map. In discussing any one aspect of the spiritual life, we must view it contextually. We have pointed out ten signs on the road to union: prayer as loving attention, prayer's relationship to love, prayer's need for discipline, prayer and proper identity, prayer's focus, the conditions for prayer, prayer's tonality, source of prayer, the principle of pluralism, and prayer's goal. A corresponding set of principles marking out other aspects of the terrain in the spiritual life could easily be worked out, and these would provide meaning in such areas as ministry and asceticism. The map is large; we have considered but one aspect. Regardless of the principle and its specification, the destination is always the same: the experience of *Love*. That experience comes alive when we move from the map to the land it describes.

1. See John 17; Rom 11:33-36.

2. *The Collected Works of St. John of the Cross*, trans. Kieran Kavanaugh, O.C.D., and Otilio Rodríguez, O.C.D. (Washington, D.C.: ICS Publications, 1973) 622.

3. Simone Weil, *Waiting for God* (New York: Harper Colophon Books, 1951) 197.

4. *The Complete Works of St. Theresa of Jesus*, ed. and trans. E. Allison Peers (London: Sheed & Ward, 1944) 2:363.

5. Rom 8:26-27.

6. 1 John 2:9-11; Luke 4:42-44.

7. Samuel Taylor Coleridge, "The Rime of the Ancient Mariner."

8. Murray Bodo, *Francis: The Journey and the Dream* (Cincinnati: St. Anthony Messenger Press, 1972) 64.

9. *The Complete Works of St. Theresa of Jesus* 2:347.

10. John 2.

11. *Spiritual Renewal of the American Priesthood* (Washington, D.C.: Publications Office, United States Catholic Conference, 1973) 48.

12. Gal 5:16-26; Matt 4:1-17.

13. *The Complete Works of St. Theresa of Jesus* 2:16.

14. *The Collected Works of St. John of the Cross* 364.

15. François Roustang, S.J., *Growth in the Spirit*, trans. Kathleen Pond (New York: Sheed & Ward, 1966) 232.

16. C. S. Lewis, *The Last Battle* (New York: Collier Books, 1956) 13.

17. Judg 6:13; Rom 7:14-25. This principle of prayer was presented in a guided retreat by Fr. William A. M. Peters, S.J.

18. *Raïssa's Journal*, presented by Jacques Maritain (Albany, N.Y.: Magi Books, 1963) 225.

19. C. S. Lewis, *Surprised by Joy* (New York: Harcourt, Brace & World, 1955) 21.

20. *The Complete Works of St. Theresa of Jesus* 1:48.

21. John H. Brennecke and Robert G. Amick, *Psychology: Understanding Yourself* (Beverly Hills, Calif.: Benziger, Bruce & Glencoe, 1975) 43.

22. C. S. Lewis, *A Grief Observed* (New York: Seabury Press, 1961) 52.

23. Ps 23; Gal 2:17-21.

24. *Raïssa's Journal*, 83.

25. Simone Weil 50–51.

26. Fynn, *Mister God, This Is Anna* (New York: Holt, Rinehart & Winston, 1974) 174.

27. George Herbert, "The Pulley."

28. Luke 22:39-46; Matt 6:5-6.

29. *The Collected Works of St. John of the Cross* 623.

30. Caryll Houselander, quoted in Maisie Ward, *Caryll Houselander: That Divine Eccentric* (New York: Sheed & Ward, 1962) 279.

31. "Circles," *Essays of Ralph Waldo Emerson* (New York: The Book League of America, 1941) 106.

32. Isa 6:1-9; Ps 118:5-7.

33. *Julian of Norwich: Showings*, translated from the critical text with an introduction by Edmund Colledge, O.S.A., and James Walsh, S.J. (New York: Paulist Press, 1978) 253.

34. Elizabeth Barrett Browning, "Aurora Leigh."

35. *Bonaventure: The Soul's Journey into God*, trans. Ewert Cousins (New York: Paulist Press, 1978) 55–56.

36. *Julian of Norwich: Showings* 159.

37. *Ibid.* 136.

38. Ps 138; John 6:44.

39. Fr. Armand Nigro's "Prayer" (source unknown).

40. *The Collected Works of St. John of the Cross* 517.

41. *Ibid.* 620.

42. *Ibid.* 232.

43. Romano Guardini, *The Life of Faith*, trans. John Chapin (Westminster, Md.: Newman Press, 1961) 106.

44. Col 3:12-17; Luke 4:42-44.

45. *The Complete Works of St. Theresa of Jesus* 2:307-308.

46. *Ibid.* 69.

47. *The Collected Works of St. John of the Cross* 633.

48. Hans Urs von Balthasar, *Prayer*, trans. A. V. Littledale (New York: Sheed & Ward, 1961) 108.

49. Ps 139; Jer 31:31-34.

50. *The Collected Works of St. John of the Cross* 523.

51. Henri J. M. Nouwen, *The Genesee Diary: Report from a Trappist Monastery* (New York: Doubleday & Co., 1976) 51.

52. William Blake, "The Little Black Boy."

7

Presence and Prayer
The ERRA Principle of Prayer

Hidden beneath the immediate vision of the human person are the underlying principles that govern, direct, support and explain the divers movements of life. The clearer our perception and understanding of these principles, the more meaning we bring to the events of our personal existence.

A principle that underlies a major portion of existence is what I call the ERRA principle. This principle involves first of all the fact of experience (E): an experience being a happening, an event, a phenomenon. It can be active (hitting a ball) or passive (being hit); an experience can be personal (it happens in my life) or vicarious (I experience death through a character in a novel); it can be particular (this time-place) or universal (applies to all).

The second element in the principle is reflection (R). This is the moment when one begins to ask questions about the experience (E). It is a time of searching for meaning, seeking to discover interrelationships, desiring insight and understanding. Every mythology, theology, philosophy and sociology is basically a reflection upon various life experiences from a certain point of view. These interpretations will depend upon one's view of man, reality and history. If the reflection is to be honest, one must have an open mind and a willingness to face the experience as it is. It should be noted that it is possible that a person might reach this level of reflection infrequently: all of one's time might be taken up with going from one experience to another, e.g., taking in a triple feature at the theater. If this is the case, an old axiom might be heeded: "An experience unreflected upon dehumanizes."

Moving from the experiential and reflective levels, the third element of the ERRA principle is response (R). One's response is primarily on the affective level just as reflection results from cognitive behavior. A response indicates a strong feeling-impulse-inclination which either affirms (is attracted by) the experience reflected upon or negates (is repulsed by) such an event. Such words as *wonderful, great, delightful, terrible, awful* characterize some responses. The third element of our principle stresses the necessity of going beyond the cerebral and possibly cold intellectuality which tends to remove much of the warmth of life. To live fully we must feel deeply and allow compassion and empathy wide movement within our hearts. Experiencing life demands both our minds and our hearts. It should be noted that it is possible simply to experience and respond to various life events without taking time to reflect on them. The danger here is that meaning is thereby excluded and our response has no firm foundation. Another possibility is that there be no response, just an experience followed by abstract reflection, not allowing the event to penetrate our affectivity. The inhumanness that results needs no comment.

If a person goes through the experience, reflection and response (ERR) dimensions of our principle, there is the possibility of a fourth element: articulation (A). This, however, depends on the acquisition, often painful and lengthy, of certain skills and techniques, e.g., artistic, musical, literary. The articulation is the moment in which a person gathers together his or her reflection and response to his or her own experiences and *shares* them with someone. Examples of this completed process are many: a gentle song, an art work, the Valentine card made by a first grader, a piece of poetry. What was implicit is now made explicit. What was on the inside gets to the outside. The process of incarnation, enfleshing reality, once again takes place. The miracle is complete when this articulation allows another person to undergo the same type of experience with similar meaning and affection. Further, the possibility of a new and richer articulation also exists for the enjoyment of still others.

Prayer as Experience

One of the great religious experiences of history was the Exodus. God's breaking through the bonds of slavery to form a people in freedom was a crucial moment in Israel's history. This communal experience gave a sense of identity, provided a trust and faith, and was to be a touchstone of God's fidelity and kindness. This prototype phenomenon in which freedom was given and bondage was ended speaks to every age.

Life is a series of experiences. Life itself can become a prayer for the person of faith who sees in so many of life's experiences the workings of God. Prayer need not be segregated only to a certain time or place; St. Paul would have us pray always. In faith all is gift and, for the person who has this level of awareness, prayer can become a way of life. The Pauline injunction that "we live through love in his presence" means that all is done in the presence of the Father.

The experiences of life are varied: we gaze at the stars and flowers of creation; we know ourselves as recipients of so many good things; we inflict injury on our brothers and sisters; we wallow in our poverty with hands outstretched. These experiences are the foundations of wonder and praise, of thanksgiving and gratitude, of sorrow and guilt, of petition and need. It seems strange that a person could simply experience some phenomenon and not move on to these acts. Yet, through the maladies of blindness and deafness, we can be present geographically to so much of life and not be there in the fullness of our person. The words of T. S. Eliot capture the danger of surface living, of the perennial temptation merely to drift along:

> We are the hollow men
> We are the stuffed men
> Leaning together
> Headpiece filled with straw. Alas!
> Our dried voices, when
> We whisper together
> Are quiet and meaningless
> As wind in dry grass. . . .

To experience deeply, however painful and risky this may be, is necessary for prayer. Depth living demands presence, surrender and openness. Lack of self-preoccupation and self-consciousness will also be prerequisites. A sensitivity to the deeper levels of life is required—no surface drifting here! In the midst of so many life experiences the Lord is calling and drawing us into his mission of reconciliation. To live at this level is to enter into experiential-existential prayer.

Prayer as Reflection

Reflection implies that we step back from our experiences to search out their meaning and significance. This intellectual process will necessarily fail to grasp completely the mystery of life. Yet there is an obligation to sort out the true from the false, the important from the unimportant, the essential from the accidental. Not every experience is of or from God. Not every experience is part of the kingdom. Not every experience is growth-oriented. The disciplined and painstaking task of examining and comparing our lived experiences is the work of our God-given minds. There is no room in Christianity for anti-intellectualism.

For some, reflection is equated with meditation, the process of thinking *about* the experiences of Christ and our own lives. To meditate on these events is to derive insight and vision. In his work *Justice*, Josef Pieper put it well: "Fundamental truths must constantly be pondered anew lest they lose their fruitfulness. In this lies the significance of meditation: that truth may not cease to be present and effective in the active life." This will require that time and energy be set aside specifically for this purpose. It is a value judgment and indeed a costly one. Not to do it, however, means paying an unendurable price: the loss of truth, or at least, its clarity.

Our Lord was a reflective person. He not only experienced life to the full, but often withdrew to ponder the past and prepare for the future. His thoughtfulness is evidenced in his prayers of thanksgiving. Alone with the disciples, he explains (reflects meaning) the details of the parables. As a young boy, he theologizes for the doctors in the temple on the inner depths of his Father's word.

To think is one form of prayer. John Macquarrie's essay, "Prayer is Thinking," emphasizes this style of prayer. For some people, this form is central; for others, it is less meaningful and they will opt for another style more suitable to their stage of growth or position in life. However, without falling into the extreme of over-intellectualizing prayer, some time must be given to reflect on the God-experiences of life. This reflection is a stepping stone to an ever deeper form of prayer.

An example of scriptural reflective prayer is as follows: as Jesus walked along the road to Emmaus after his resurrection, why did he appear as a pilgrim? Why did he ask questions about matters he already knew? What passages did he probably interpret for the two disciples? Why did Jesus pretend he was going on? What was the risen Lord really like? Does this same Lord come and go within our contemporary time? Reverent mental probing of the mysteries of our Lord's life is a deep form of prayer. Before our gaze is the God-man:

and whoever sees Jesus, sees the Father. This meditation leads us to a deeper knowledge of the Father in the Spirit. Reflective prayer presupposes that the Spirit will enlighten our mental faculties so that, even though it seems that we are doing all the work, real prayer always begins in the Lord, is accomplished in the Spirit, and terminates in the glory and praise of the Father. Otherwise, it might turn out to be a fruitless exercise of fulfilling a duty which ends in little other than mental fatigue.

Whatever leads to truth must be reverenced. Our intellects lead to cognitive union with the Lord when his presence dominates our consciousness. Though there is a danger of overinvolvement in our role through reflection, it is a necessary preparation for more passive-listening forms of dialogue with God.

Prayer as Response

Response implies a felt affirmation or negation of a reflected-upon experience. Though the reflection itself is a type of response, the concentration here is on the affective level—what happens in the heart concerning this experience.

A person of faith strives to find God in every situation of life. If the process of discernment is well developed, one is able to come to terms with the ultimate origin of an event or happening. To stop at the gift and not proceed to the giver is to respond superficially. It is being caught by appearances and not perceiving the basic reality. The Christian is called upon to sense God in the multiple facets of creation. St. Paul, having *felt* God in so many divers ways, urges:

> Fill your minds with everything that is true, everything that is noble, everything that is good and pure, everything that we love and honor, and everything that can be thought virtuous or worthy of praise. . . . Then the God of peace will be with you (Phil 4:8-9).

Perhaps the most intense reponse we can make is that of intimacy. Prayer as response is an invitation simply to be with the Lord who is behind all experience and revealed in profound reflection. We are invited to be embraced by his gaze, drawn into his peace, held by his joy. Such an encounter led the psalmist to sing, "Apart from you I have no good" (Ps 16).

The God of intimacy speaks to the heart of every individual through the prophet Isaiah:

> Do not be afraid, for I have redeemed you;
> I have called you by your name, you are mine.

. . . you are precious in my eyes,
because you are honored and I love you,
I give men in exchange for you,
peoples in return for your life.
Do not be afraid, for I am with you (43:1b, 4-5).

God's response to us is one of love and forgiveness, one of longing to share himself with us and to draw us to share ourselves with him. This mutual intimacy corresponds to the classical description of prayer as contemplation, a form of loving knowledge.

Two things radically affect one's style of prayer: one's temperament, and the presence or absence of certain traits of character. Every individual has certain biological and psychological dispositions which condition the intensity of his or her affectivity as well as the basic pattern of life itself. Some personalities are extremely warm and personable; their form of prayer fits in well with prayer as response. Others, having a temperament of a more intellectual and less affective bent, might turn to prayer as reflection as the most satisfactory communication with God. Since our temperaments are mixtures and blends of many different elements, all of the various prayer forms might come into play at different times in our development. The crucial role of temperament in prayer indicates the importance of self-knowledge. Only frustration can result when a person of one temperament takes as a model the prayer life of someone of an entirely different background.

Certain traits of character also play their significant role in prayer as response. To mention but a few: openness, sensitivity, surrender, compassion, sympathy. These positive traits provide fertile soil for the seed of God's word to sprout and bear much fruit. Opposite qualities are obviously major obstacles to communication with God: hostility, narrow-mindedness, cold-heartedness. Jeremiah the prophet points out the basic components of character necessary for a deep and authentic response—a new mind and a new heart. Once again we see God as the very source of any real prayer life. The Spirit makes us capable of entering into intimate oneness with the Father and the Son.

It is not polite to eavesdrop on affective dialogue unless invited to do so. St. Augustine shares with us a precious example of prayer as response when he writes:

Late have I loved Thee, O Beauty so ancient and so new; late have I loved Thee! For behold thou wert within me, and I outside; and I sought Thee outside and in my unloveliness fell upon those lovely things that Thou has made. Thou wert with me and I was not with Thee. I was kept from Thee by those things, yet had they not been in Thee, they would not have been at all. Thou didst call and cry to me and break open my deafness: and Thou didst send forth Thy beams and shine upon me and chase away my blindness: Thou didst breathe fragrance upon me, and I drew in my breath and do now pant for Thee: I tasted Thee, and now hunger and thirst for Thee: Thou didst touch me, and I have burned for Thy peace (*Confessions,* bk. X, ch. 27).

Prayer as Articulation

A loving husband who has had a successful business adventure looks forward to sharing this experience with his wife. As he reflects and anticipates with delight the interest of his partner, we see the completion of the ERRA principle. In the telling (articulation) of his latest accomplishment, the wife can now vicariously enter into the original experience and the joy is doubled.

Prayer as articulation follows the same pattern. We verbalize what the Father has been doing within our lives. The psalms are splendid examples of articulations of experiences reflected upon and responded to. Articulation embodies the thoughts and feelings that surface from the "peak experiences" of life, making them now available to other pilgrims. Sometimes, because of the nature of the experience and its personal intimacy, the articulation takes place in solitude, available only to God in fitting praise and worship. Liturgy as such is an articulation in words and gestures of spiritual realities. This articulation allows the community to participate in the experience of the good news.

The poetry of Gerard Manley Hopkins offers many examples of articulated prayer. In his "Pied Beauty" we can sense the depth of his experience of God, the perceptiveness of his thought, the intensity of his feelings, and the powerful skills of verbal sharing:

> Glory be to God for dappled things—
> For skies of couple-colour as a brinded cow;
> For rose-moles all in stipple upon trout that swim;
> Fresh-firecoal chestnut-fails; finches' wings;
> Landscape plotted and pieced—fold, fallow, and plough;
> And all trades, their gear and tackle and trim.
>
> All things counter, original, spare, strange;
> Whatever is fickle, freckled (who knows how?)

With swift, slow; sweet, sour; adazzle, dim;
He fathers-forth whose beauty is past change:
Praise him.

This form of prayer will not be predominant for everyone. Sharing demands both the development of certain technical skills and a growth of personality allowing for deep dialogue. These circumstances having been met, the miracle of dialogue takes place wherever there is sensitive listening, openness to new happenings and a desire for growth. In such cases, the treasury of our tradition, so rich in its wealth of articulated prayers, leads to new and surprising encounters with the living and true God.

The ERRA principle (experience-reflection-reponse-articulation) is an artificial construct from which to view various forms and kinds of prayer. Needless to say, one form is not necessarily better than another. Each has its advantages as well as its limitations. The important thing in prayer, regardless of style or method, is that we come before the living God in deep faith and worship. God's role is always central. He longs to reveal the good news of his Son; its reception into our minds and hearts brings about a transformation of infinite proportions. A danger in our times is to lose perspective, to be so bombarded by a multiplicity of experiences that we fail adequately to reflect upon and respond to any of them, with the result that there is nothing (no one) to share. ERRA is presented with the hope that our prayer may become more existential, more thought-filled, more loving, and more sharable.

8

Presence and Peace
Integration and Reconciliation

Integration is concerned with "putting it all together." This admirable quality is sometimes ascribed to actresses who excel in their art, to professional athletes who have reached the peak of performance, to persons who live healthy, balanced lives. How common or rare these people are is a matter of dispute. Perhaps most of us could identify, not so much with the integrated universal man of the Renaissance, but rather with the plight of poor Humpty-Dumpty. Like him, all the king's horses and all the king's men cannot quite get us put back together again. The fragmented life of Humpty-Dumpty is a universal image in that all people of every age have had to contend with the realities of division, alienation and anomie. These forces are strangers to no one, though the intensity and longevity of each varies from person to person. Lest we despair in the face of this disintegrative factor of reality, we must also come to recognize that the process of healing is a significant power in life. The healing process mends and restores persons, relationships and the world. A realistic view of life demands that the dialectical nature of division and healing, sin and grace, sickness and health all be fully appreciated for what they are.

Despite the fact of disintegration, the Christian vocation has as its goal both individual and communal wholeness: integration in love is God's call to mankind. Our trust and hope is grounded in the Spirit of love who unifies and heals all of life. This love, God's gift of himself to his people, draws us into an intimacy with him that is the core of Christian living. Like a fish in water or like a bird in the air, the very

91

existence of the Christian demands the presence of God's love. St. Paul's message to the Ephesians summarizes this so well (1:4): "To live through love in his presence." God's love is the source of all integration; living outside that love results in the darkness and estrangement flowing from separation from the source of light and peace. Those who have traveled before us have expressed well the central role of God in human life: the psalmist prayed, "You are my God. My happiness lies in you alone" (Ps 16). Augustine also summarized the nature of true peace: "For thou hast made us for thyself and our hearts are restless till they rest in thee."

The succinct call to integration comes from Scripture: "This is what Yahweh asks of you: only this, to act justly, to love tenderly and to walk humbly with your God" (Mic 6:8). Though we smile at the slight understatement ("only this"), the prophet presents a vision of life that is radically simple. The complexity of intricate theologies, the score of duties and obligations, the multiplicity of laws all seem less threatening when we can summarize God's will in terms of being and becoming a just, loving and faithful person and people. These qualities reveal the interiority of integration. Justice leads to peace and oneness, whereas injustice, by withholding from others their proper due, causes division. Love unifies through affirmation and support, thus providing hope to the weary and discouraged, whereas apathy and indifference isolate and separate person from person. Faith, the intimacy of a personal relationship with Christ, is an integrative power shedding light and warmth on the human spirit, while faithlessness terminates in the despair of meaninglessness. Justice, love and faith are seen as the ingredients of an integrated existence.

The sacrament of reconciliation aims at fostering the vocation common to all of us: to-be-one with God, with others, with the world and with ourselves. As do all the other sacraments, the sacrament of reconciliation makes present God's love and forgiveness in a special way. Through the encounter with Christ, the penitent is offered the grace of healing, which helps to put back together again all the spiritual Humpty Dumptys of history, and we are in that number. God's gracious love hurries to mend the deep split within the person which Paul Tillich describes so well:

> It is important to remember that we are not merely separated from each other. For we are also separated from ourselves. *Man Against Himself* is not merely the title of a book, but rather also indicates the rediscovery of an age-old insight. Man is split within himself. . . .

But the depth of our separation lies in just the fact that we are not capable of a great and merciful divine love towards ourselves.[1]

It is in Jesus that this divine and merciful love touches our lives to make us whole once again.

Integration: Personal and Communal—The HHH Principle

The historical pendulum swings violently from one extreme to the other. One period will stress the uniqueness of the individual without giving proper attention to the social nature of the person. The rugged individualism of American history is a case in point. Then the pendulum, having reached its one extreme, swings its reactionary way to the other pole. Collectivism and totalitarian ideologies arise to stress the social whole to the exclusion of individual rights. The twentieth century's political and social theories of fascism and communism are examples of this one-sided mentality.

The truth of the matter lies in the middle: both the individual and the social facets of human existence must be recognized, protected and fostered. Their interdependence and interrelatedness are principles of integral living. Oneness involves both the individual person and the community. The new rites for celebrating the sacrament of reconciliation carefully protect both dimensions. This fact must be kept in mind throughout the following description of integration. The themes and principles of integration applicable to the individual are also, by way of analogy, necessary for an understanding of communal integration.

On the personal level, there are three major elements seeking integration. Anatomically, each of us has a *head*, a *heart*, and *hands* (HHH). Symbolically, these parts of the human body represent the capacity to know, to feel and to act. In the field of education, the concern for growth of the whole person is spoken of in terms of developing the cognitive, affective and behavioral domains. On a community level, these elements might be described as common beliefs, common sentiments and a common life-style. Insofar as there is harmony (congruence) among these various components, there is a sense of integration and peace; when these elements contradict each other or are unrelated, the result will be one of varying degrees of conflict and tension.

Looking more closely at the personal level, we can discover the interrelationships among the various elements seeking integration. Through cognitive powers we search out the truth, often at a high cost. Cardinal Newman speaks of one "who has given up much that he loved and prized and could have retained, but that he loved honesty better than name, and Truth better than dear friends."[2] The consequence of living in the truth, as St. John's Gospel points out, is that it leads to freedom: the truth makes us free while ignorance enslaves and issues in fears. We were born to see reality in its deepest dimensions and to act on the knowledge discovered there. Carl Jung in his autobiography shares a universal principle that deals with the relationship between knowledge and action: "It is equally a grave mistake to think that it is enough to gain the understanding of the images and that knowledge can here make a halt. Insight into them must be converted into an ethical obligation."[3] It is through the cognitive capacities of reason and intuition that insights emerge, concepts and principles are formulated, conclusions are drawn and life is lived. Our creeds, constitutions, journals and discourses attempt to record our mental travels. Though our perceptions are always limited and our articulations fail to capture the fulness of the reality, yet the extent of our knowledge is amazingly vast.

The affective domain, symbolized by the heart, takes us into a rich though complex area of life. Feelings, emotions, urges, tendencies, and drives are terms attempting to describe some of the powerful and ambiguous movements of our affectivity. Here it is that joy and sorrow, panic and calm, anxiety and peace are experienced in degrees which only our unique person can narrate. Because literature claims for its own the matters of the heart, it has universal appeal. So often the literary genius speaks of the affective level. "When your own heart's been broken it will be time for you to think of talking."[4] "I do not know at all,' said Martin. 'I should have to be in your heart to know.'"[5]

The relationship between the cognitive and affective domain is complex. During certain periods of life a dichotomy exists between the two. (One calculation measured the distance from head to heart to be two light years!) How many Christians know intellectually that God loves them and is always present to them and yet do not experience this truth in their hearts? Possession of an accurate and sound theology does not guarantee an experience of the heart. With integration between intellectual conviction and personal affectivity, the distance seems to vanish and there is a mutual support and affirmation. Emerson's insight is profound: "Our intellectual and active powers increase with our affection."[6] Truth experienced affectively and affections experienced in truth enrich life.[7]

The old line, "Do as I say, not as I do!" draws attention to the third ingredient in personal and communal life: behavior. The question arises: do the words that I speak and the action I perform truly express what is in my mind and heart? Do I live out my beliefs and values? Disintegration is experienced when a discrepancy exists between what I know to be true intellectually and a life-style that contradicts that truth, or when a discrepancy arises between that life-style and what I am feeling at the gut level. Every day life provides examples of such discrepancies: to know that a certain substance, such as alcohol, is dangerous in certain quantities and yet continue to drink; to prize physical fitness as an important value and yet never take time to exercise; to yearn for intimacy with a loving God and never take time for prayer. Integration is realized when we channel into behavior our limited time and energy in such a way that this behavior parallels our thinking and feeling. A single stream is formed, a stream that contains truth, beauty and goodness.

Integration and the Sacrament of Reconciliation

The new rite of the sacrament of reconciliation delineates four basic and essential components: contrition, confession, satisfaction and absolution. These four elements directly foster both personal and communal integration. The sacrament is the means by which the Lord Jesus makes us whole, healing the division within each person and the communal fragmentation resulting from injustice and apathy. The new rite speaks to the head, the heart and the hands—to the whole person.

In the new ritual, *contrition* is described as "a profound change of the whole person by which one begins to consider, judge and arrange his life according to the holiness and love of God" (Ritual, #6). This is a call to integration, to put our lives together with God's help and to continue to grow in his gracious love. This process of growth implies an openness to God's word which transforms and molds us. It means that, as a pilgrim people, our lives are always in process and stand in need of conversion. Minimal self-knowledge exposes the dark areas of our life where selfishness flourishes and superficial change predominates. The new rite speaks of contrition as something that goes down to the very depths of our person, radically touching our ideas, attitudes and conduct. Integration is possible only at this level.

Though conversion is a gradual process involving grace, time and energy, it is not meant to be piecemeal. God calls the whole person, not just one aspect of life. This realization helps to protect the unity of the person and implies that what affects one area of life will affect, if not immediately at least eventually, every other area. The ritual spells out the process of conversion as it touches upon three components of integration explained earlier: 1) *Consideration.* We are challenged to use our cognitive abilities to consider how our personal and communal lives measure up to the holiness and love of God. 2) *Judgment.* After deliberation, we draw conclusions about how to improve our response to God and his will, employing the richness of our affectivity to sustain and give dynamism to that response. 3) *Arranging life.* Authentic contrition means that our life-style, what we say and how we say it, the kinds and quality of our relationships, and our reaching out to others, must at certain points be adjusted and modified. This broad, panoramic view of contrition challenges both the inner and outer person. The sacrament of reconciliation calls the whole person to turn to the living and true God in hope and fidelity.

Confession, the second main component in the new rite, "comes from true knowledge of self before God and from contrition for those sins" (Ritual, #6). Our sacramental system, concerned as it is with the covenant relationship between God and man, is obviously person-centered. It involves our worship of the person of our gracious Father, a deep participation in the paschal mystery of our Lord Jesus, the giftedness of peace and joy flowing from the Spirit. The trinitarian God is the core of all the sacraments. The challenge is to come to an even deeper knowledge of the living God, and from this perspective, to achieve our true identity. The crucial role of the Scriptures becomes obvious in this framework. In God's word we find the revelation of his love and forgiveness; we enter into the rich world of faith. Cognitively we discover the reality of God's love, which is the truth that creates freedom. Experiential knowledge of this most central fact necessarily touches the deepest affections of the heart. We are stirred interiorly to respond with our whole lives to this gaze of love. The canticle of Mary is a confession of being loved:

> My soul proclaims the greatness of the Lord,
> my spirit rejoices in God my savior
> for he has looked with favor on his lowly servant (Luke 1:46).

True affective knowledge works its way into the behavioral domain. Our life becomes different; our words and deeds originate from the wellspring of God's mercy and goodness. The confessing of sins will thus involve the whole person: what we know, what we feel, what we have done and will do. Confessing both expresses and promotes integration.

Satisfaction or the act of penance is the third important element in the new rite. In a special way satisfaction reaches beyond the notion of personal integration to embrace the larger community. In doing the truth, in correcting injustices, in serving more deeply, we implicitly call others to witness and experience the newly gained integration of our own lives. The Roman Ritual states: "True conversion is completed by acts of penance or satisfaction for the sins committed, by amendment of conduct, by reparation of injury . . . to restore order" (Ritual, #6c). Integration implies and necessitates order. Wholeness exists when things are in place just as fragmentation is experienced in chaos. In a sense, sin is being "out of place." In Gibson's play *The Miracle Worker*, Annie Sullivan, the teacher of Helen Keller, speaks to herself in a mirror: "Don't worry. They'll find you, you're not lost. Only out of place." The "hound of heaven" pursues us when we lose our way in the darkness of sin; when the Lord captures us with his mercy and love, he relocates us in the plan of the Father.

For true satisfaction we must be aware and understand that the proper order of things has been broken (cognitive element); we must interiorly feel and be concerned about the anguish and restlessness caused by sin in our lives and the lives of those we touch (affective element); with God's grace we must reconstruct the harmony shattered by our infidelity (behavorial element). This whole process of reconciliation is no abstract, nebulous role playing; it touches the core of our lives. It is based on fact and experience. Though somewhat overstated, Carl Jung's reflection that "in religious matters only experience counted" does express the seriousness surrounding the sacrament of reconciliation. Satisfaction, the acting out of heartfelt sorrow in experience, is a vital integrative force restoring that order that leads to justice and peace.

Absolution is the fourth main element in the celebration of God's mercy. The new formula of absolution contains a wealth of theology, deserving in its own right a detailed explication. The minister, representing the risen Lord and the Church, prays:

> God, the Father of mercies,
> through the death and resurrection of his Son,
> has reconciled the world to himself
> and sent the Holy Spirit among us

for the forgiveness of sins;
through the ministry of the Church
may God give you pardon and peace.
And I absolve you from your sins
in the name of the Father, and of the Son,
and of the Holy Spirit. Amen.

The whole person is drawn to respond to this majestic oration. The mind is nourished with the experience of a merciful God, with the marvel of the paschal mystery, with the fact of the instrumentality of the Church, with the knowledge that pardon and peace are gifts from God, with the understanding that all three persons of the Trinity heal the sickness of the person. These insights liberate us from false fears and narrow slaveries, enlighten the darkness of our minds, enrich our faith, and foster wisdom, allowing us to see what is truly essential and worthwhile. Our affectivity is also nourished by this prayer of absolution. Our heart is touched by the revelation of God's love and graciousness, by the joy of reconciliation, by the dispelling of anxiety and guilt, by the calmness of peace and pardon. The sacrament intends to soften the hardness of heart and to foster the gentleness that alone brings life. Full, active and conscious participation in this encounter with the risen Lord abets a richer affective life. Integration proves itself in action, and the prayer of absolution necessarily includes Christian living; it touches the transformation of our truths and feelings into words and deeds. The absolution formula provides an example of what forgiveness is, thus challenging us to forgive each other as God forgives us. We are called to participate in the death-resurrection of Christ in our daily lives, dying to our selfishness in being for others. Through the gift of the Spirit, we are empowered to enrich the world by sharing the Spirit's love, joy and peace. Our lives are different when we recognize experientially the price of our sins: the cross. The shadow of the cross calls us to repent and to believe. The prayer of absolution is a prayer leading us to authenticity. It provides the vision that harmonizes our visible life of daily conduct with the new mind and heart we have put on in Christ.

Integration and the Holy Spirit

The possibility of Christian integration is based on the gift of Spirit. The risen Lord in union with the Father sends their spirit into the world to complete the work of redemption. Through the sacrament of reconciliation this work of restoration takes on visibility and becomes efficacious in the lives of those who believe. The Spirit directs us in our struggle toward oneness within ourselves and among all people. Within the framework of the HHH Principle, we can examine the role of the Spirit in the process of integration.

The tradition of the Church points out that there are four gifts of the Spirit that aid the intellectual and faith growth of God's people: wisdom, knowledge, counsel and understanding. Through these "cognitive" gifts we contend with the ever-present forces of folly, ignorance, rashness and dullness of mind. God, coming to the aid of our finite minds, supplements our ability to grasp truth through the personal light of his presence.

The heart, often bruised and broken, also stands in need of special gifts. Through the Pentecost event, fortitude, piety and fear of the Lord are offered as powerful nutrients enriching our affectivity. Thus we are enabled to stand firm in the face of fear, to struggle valiantly against hardness of heart and *acedia*, to deal honestly with the arrogance of pride seeking to remove God from the center of life. In the sacrament of reconciliation, these gifts are available with the coming of the Spirit.

But discernment is a difficult task in life. How do we know whether or not we are growing in the Lord? Are we really allowing the mind and heart of Christ to influence our lives? What are the signs of health and illness in our Christian lives? Through the writings of St. Paul, God has given us an evaluation system to aid us in testing the quality of Christian growth. In his letter to the Galatians, Paul spells out the evidence indicating the spirit of evil and the Spirit of God. If the signs of God's Spirit are present, we have some assurance that we are doing the will of the Father and that the gifts of the Spirit are truly effective in our words and deeds. If the opposite signs are present, we are provided with some hard evidence that we are failing in our Christian responsibilities. Paul writes:

> But when you follow your own wrong inclinations your lives will produce these evil results: impure thoughts, eagerness for lustful pleasure, idolatry, hatred and fighting, jealously and anger, constant effort to get the best for yourself, complaints and criticisms, the feeling that everyone else is wrong except those in your own little group —and there will be wrong doctrine, envy, murder, drunkenness, wild parties, and all that sort of thing. . . . But when the Holy Spirit controls our lives he will produce this kind of fruit in us: love, joy, peace, patience, kindness, goodness, faithfulness, gentleness and self-control (Gal 5:19-23).

The revision of the sacrament of reconciliation provides the contemporary Church with a process and vision to bring about the oneness we all desire. Unity is something intrinsic to our lives. William Lynch beautifully expresses this need in every person:

> What I want first to propose, as a sort of working point of discussion, is that the very deepest need the people have is the need for closeness to, union with, things and persons and God. This principle underlies every need of man. It is not a luxury or a gimmick. It is fundamental, primitive, eternal and universal. . . . Everybody knows, when it is put in his language, that real solitude is hell and that unity is peace.[8]

The sacrament of reconciliation deals directly with that aspect of our life which obstructs and prohibits unity: the reality of sin. The great marvel is that God's love and mercy have conquered sin and death and through the sacrament of reconciliation bring us in touch with this victory of God.

A schematic summary of this chapter might appear as follows:

A. God's initiative: the call to justice
    love (lived out fully in the person of Jesus)
    faith
B. Human response: so much injustice/apathy/faithlessness (mystery of sin)
C. Jesus came to reconcile all creation to the Father—continues to come in their Spirit to heal the whole person—to bring about integration

Truth overcomes falsity	Head	Gifts of wisdom, knowledge, counsel, understanding
Beauty overcomes ugliness	Heart	Gifts of piety, fortitude, fear of the Lord
Goodness overcomes evil	Hand	Signs: love, joy, peace, patience, kindness, goodness, faithfulness, gentleness, self-control

D. Result: Oneness with the Father through Christ in the Spirit. Wholeness, union, sanctity, integration.

A growing appreciation of the depth and breadth of the sacrament of reconciliation is important if we are fully to enter into this great gift. The revised rite provides us with many advantages: the stress and variety of Scripture, the personal touch with the face-to-face option, the emphasis on the communal nature of sin, the demand for authentic conversion, the joyful tone of celebrating God's mercy and love and not getting caught up in oneself. Our challenge is to understand as fully as possible the meaning of the sacrament and to experience its tremendous force in our personal and communal lives.

1. Paul Tillich, *The Shaking of the Foundations* (New York: Charles Scribner's Sons, 1948) 158.

2. John Henry Cardinal Newman, *Apologia Pro Vita Sua* (Boston: Houghton Mifflin Company, 1956) 11.

3. C. G. Jung, *Memories, Dreams, Reflections*, recorded and edited by Aniela Jaffe, translated from the German by Richard and Clara Winston (New York: Vintage Books, Inc., 1963) 192–93.

4. C. S. Lewis, *The Great Divorce* (New York: Macmillan Publishing Co., Inc., 1946) 97.

5. *The Best Known Works of Voltaire* (New York: The Book League, 1940) 142.

6. "Friendship," *Essays of Ralph Waldo Emerson* (New York: The Book League, 1941) 65.

7. Two comments might be made at this point. Newman's well-known distinction between real and notional knowledge explains the dichotomy in more academic terms. Secondly, in light of the importance of affectivity in human and spiritual living, our educational institutions must more systematically attempt to educate the affective area of life as well as the intellectual.

8. William F. Lynch, S.J., *The Integrating Mind* (New York: Sheed and Ward, 1962) 134–35.

9

Presence and Power
Spiritual Staying Power

In teaching people the truths about his Father's kingdom, Jesus often used examples from nature: the simple sparrow, the lush lilies of the field, the unfortunate fig tree, the nonverbal clues of the sky, the miraculous yeast. Through these concrete images, deeper mysteries were unveiled opening the minds and hearts of people to the marvels of God's gracious love.

We can do no better than to fall back on nature to attempt, through the use of analogy, to ponder the multifold facets of our faith. From the world of biology comes the notion of homeostasis which can assist us in understanding the necessity of grounding our lives on solid rock. Dr. Hans Selye summarizes the essential meaning of this biological principle:

> It was the great French physiologist Claude Bernard who during the second half of the nineteenth century—well before anyone thought of stress—first pointed out clearly that the internal environment (the *milieu interieur*) of a living organism must remain fairly constant despite changes in its external environment. He realized that "it is a fixity of the *milieu interieur* which is the condition of free and inde-pendent life."
>
> Some fifty years later, the distinguished American physiologist, Walter B. Cannon, suggested that "the coordinated physiological processes which maintain most of the steady states in the organism" should be called "homeostasis" (from the Greek *homoios*, meaning similar, and *stasis*, meaning position), the ability to stay the same, or static. Homeostasis might roughly be translated as "staying power."[1]

103

The homeostatic principle, as applied to the external world, needs little documentation as to its importance due to the writings in the field of ecology. What needs considerable reflection is the importance and meaning of spiritual homeostasis, that reality in our spiritual lives which is the force enabling us to maintain a certain level of stability despite radical and oftentimes violent changes in our external environment. Spiritual homeostasis is the cultivation of a certain internal stability, developed through grace and discipline, that enables a person to "weather" the trials, temptations and sufferings of life in a reasonable manner.

Several examples from observable nature might help in understanding the notion of homeostasis. A palm tree survives the violence of a hurricane because its roots (homeostatic element) are deeply embedded in the soil; the March kite maintains a modicum of stability because of its carefully attached tail; the sailboat does not become the plaything of the strong breeze because of its rudder. Roots, a weighted rag, and a vertical board each provide stability despite elements of stress and strain. By way of comparison, each of us must face the demands of life, demands arising from within and without. If we are not to be carried away by the high winds of life, there must be some grounding element providing continuity and stability. This essay is a consideration of this grounding, of our spiritual homeostatic principle.

A note of caution is in order: the inward journey, made either to construct our inner principles or to examine the ones that already direct our lives, involves risks and the universal fears of travelers. Carl Jung wrote of these risks: "Wherever there is a reaching down into innermost experience, into the nucleus of personality, most people are overcome by fright, and many run away. . . . the risk of inner experience, the adventure of the spirit, is in any case, alien to most human beings."[2]

Of all the reasons for hesitating to make the journey, perhaps the greatest fear lies in the possibility that we will find nothing there—no homeostatic principle grounding our lives in "substance." For all our talk, reflecting and apodictic shouting, the interior could be empty—and who could live if that were true? Dante, in describing the precious coin of faith (the ultimate homeostatic principle) and its fine attributes, dares to ask the fatal question:

> Well have we examined
> The weight and alloy of this precious coin;
> But tell me if thou hast it in thy purse?[3]

Just as the kite's tail needs periodic mending, just as the sailboat's rudder needs annual repairs, just as the tree's roots need constant contact with the dark rich soil, so each of us must make our own inward journey, despite risks and fears, to examine the quality and growth of our homeostatic principle.

Let us take St. Paul as our "case study" and attempt to isolate his homeostatic principle. Even if the attempt fails, enough insight might be provided for each of us to either clarify or construct our own spiritual anchor. Pauline scholars might opt for one of the following passages as being central to Paul's spirituality, central in that all of life's experiences might be related to it for meaning and insight: "Let your thoughts be on heavenly things, and not on things that are on earth, because you have died, and now the life you have is hidden with Christ in God" (Col 3:2-3).[4] "And I live now not with my own life but with the life of Christ who lives in me" (Gal 2:20).

Though not excluding the central messages in the above two passages, my own personal choice of Paul's homeostatic principle comes from a passage in his letter to the Ephesians (1:3-4): "Blessed be God the Father of our Lord Jesus Christ, who has blessed us with all the spiritual blessings of heaven in Christ. Before the world was made, he chose us, chose us in Christ, to be holy and spotless, and *to live through love in his presence* . . ." (emphasis added). Taking as an hypothesis that "to live through love in his presence" was Paul's spiritual cable, what are some of the implications of this homeostatic principle?

To Live: Union with the Spirit

The Pepsi generation shouts out the challenge: Come alive! Whether or not a carbonated soda can achieve such a towering feat could be questioned; the challenge cannot. We are called to choose life (Deut 30:15-20), to share in the fulness of life (John 10:10), to live in justice, love and faith (Mic 6:8). Yet, because of collective and personal sin, our existences are fragmented and our potential lies dormant under piles of "shoulds," "tomorrows," and "new years." We see but do not comprehend, listen but do not understand, touch but remain unaffected. Walter Kerr sees our dilemma in this light: "If I were required to put into a single sentence my own explanation of the state of our hearts, heads, and nerves, I would do it this way: we are vaguely wretched because we are leading half-lives, halfheartedly, and with only one-half of our minds actively engaged in making contact with the universe about us."[5]

Every so often someone crosses our path whose very spirit exudes life. Sparkling eyes, a lightness of voice, gentle responses all mark a sense of meaning and motivation. A personal creativity overflows, igniting wicks and healing crushed reeds (Isa 42:3). Such a presence is anticipated with longing and remembered with joy. Such a person gives life because there is life within. A quality of transparency allows all others to taste and see life itself. In the presence of such a life-giver Hopkins' question spontaneously arises: "What is all this juice and all this joy?"

The Christian traces such a spirited life to the Spirit. God the Father and the risen Lord have sent into all creation their Spirit. Whoever receives this Spirit truly comes alive. Whoever refuses the Spirit or fails to recognize the Spirit's presence lives in darkness, half-alive, wallowing in ignorance and fear, fretting in anxieties and tears, doubting the meaning of existence. A spiritless Macbeth, no longer able to sustain his guilt, attempts to preserve a modicum of sanity by denying the meaning of life:

> Out, out brief candle!
> Life's but a walking shadow, a poor player
> That struts and frets his hour upon the stage,
> And then is heard no more; it is a tale
> Told by an idiot, full of sound and fury,
> Signifying nothing (Act V, Sc. v).

Without the Spirit darkness reigns and we curse that darkness. Life becomes a burden too difficult to bear and freedom a poisonous responsibility.

St. Paul was graced with the gift of the Spirit. To live was to be in conscious, personal union with this reality and to act from this center. Three basic forms of acting out a Spirit-transformed mind and heart include a spirit of loving attention, a spirit of joyful mortification and a spirit of courageous action. Aliveness in Paul's life embraces a balanced life of prayer, asceticism and apostolate, all flowing from his being loved by God and attempting to love in return. The quality and tonality of the response is crucial. Each of these three areas, though of significance in and of itself, is entirely different when shared in fellowship with the Spirit and is essentially a response to a personal invitation to communicate with, to suffer with, and to work with the Spirit of the Father and the Son. This divine companionship doubles all the victories in building up the kingdom and halves the apparent defeats.

Spirit of *loving attention.* It is possible to be attentive to someone or something without love. The hostile stare or the crowded "person-less" elevator ride are two instances. A vague love is also possible, unable to center on a defined object: "I love humanity but find it dif-ficult to love individual people." Such forms of attentiveness and unspecified love do not allow us to live fully. God's Spirit draws us to truly see, perceive, comprehend the creation in which we live. Paus-ing to be embraced by a spring flower, stopping suddenly to be swept heavenward by a starry night, being swept off one's feet by a warm night breeze are strains of deeper mysteries and realities. So many layers blocking our sensitivity must be penetrated if we are to be touched by outside realities; so much cluttering has made us inatten-tive to the voices of friends and the needs of the wounded. Poets are eternal prophets calling all of us to attention, to a loving attention of truth and beauty:

> Look at the stars! Look, look up at the skies!
> O look at all the fire-folk sitting in the air![6]

The homeostatic principle ("to love . . .") in the life of St. Paul con-tained a deep love and a profound concentration as he journeyed through life. Because of this not only the man but his writings are so alive.

Spirit of *joyful mortification.* Paradoxically life embraces death, self-actualization of necessity involves self-denial. Without reflecting on this phenomenon, most of us would have to struggle to accept the complementarity of the living-dying mystery. Yet if we glance for a moment into the lives of people who have evidenced life to the full, we come across the fact of much voluntary suffering and dying. Teresa of Avila, called by God to reform her religious community, freely accepted the ridicule and harassment that went along with this leadership role; Thomas More, requested by his king to sign his name to a document which would mean that his life would be spared, freely accepted death rather than lose his integrity and be unfaithful to his God; Cardinal Newman, drawn to the Roman Catholic Church, fol-lowed his religious belief in the face of the pain of being alienated from friends and kin by such a decision. In each case there was tremendous suffering; in each case there was new, powerful life. The demands were not limited to a giving of one's time and energy, rare commodities in themselves, but a giving on a much deeper level: the giving of oneself. A denial of self for the sake of life we identify as mortification.

Is it possible to speak of *joyful* mortification? Two considerations come to mind. First, there is joy in the act of mortification because the focus rests not on the suffering, though it is the immediate fact, but centers on the life that comes through the self-denial. Had Teresa of Avila dwelt on the sneers and raised eyebrows of some members of her order, her call to reformation could well have been delayed for some time; had Thomas More dwelt on the pain of execution, his commitment to the truth might have been threatened; if Cardinal Newman had centered on the anguish and affliction resulting from separating himself from so many dear friends, his conversion would have become increasingly difficult. The secret of their ability to deny themselves and accept the price of asceticism was a vision of the good that would be achieved. "Joy is the knowledge that we possess something that is good" (Abbot Marmion). And though the good may well be miles down the road and a matter of long-range consequences, those who see are enabled to deny themselves joyfully.

A second, more powerful and more personal reason for joy lies in the fact that Christians practice mortification in union with the Lord. Just as Jesus suffered freely in reconciling the world to the Father, so too Christians must pick up the cross voluntarily if they truly desire to share in the risen life. Failure to suffer in union with Christ means the risk of self-righteousness, false pride and inevitable sadness. The grace needed is the generosity to do all things in Christ. Our fasting, our giving of time, our withholding that "brilliant insight"[7] so that others might be free to speak are all forms of denying self, but in conjunction with the Lord. Joy results in sharing life together—whether that embraces health or illness, success or failure, peace or conflict— the important thing being the mutuality and not the positive or negative experience. Mortification takes on full reality as one means of participation in the life of Christ. This fellowship, this participation, is the source of our joy.

St. Paul's aliveness is characterized by both joy and mortification. His letters to the early Christian churches, permeated with so much suffering yet with an extravagant generosity, provide us with sufficient evidence that Paul might well be a paradigm for all aspiring ascetics:

> For I am certain of this: neither death nor life, no angel, no prince, nothing that exists, nothing still to come, not any power, or height or depth, nor any created thing, can ever come between us and the love of God made visible in Christ Jesus our Lord (Rom 8:38-39).

We are only the earthenware jars that hold this treasure, to make it clear that such an overwhelming power comes from God and not from us. We are in difficulties on all sides, but never cornered; we see no answer to our problem, but never despair; we have been persecuted, but never deserted; knocked down, but never killed; always, wherever we may be, we carry with us in our body the death of Jesus, so that the life of Jesus, too, may always be seen in our body. Indeed, while we are still alive, we are consigned to our death every day, for the sake of Jesus, so that in our mortal flesh the life of Jesus, too, may be openly shown. So death is at work in us, but life in you (2 Cor 4:7-12).

Paul's homeostatic principle dealt directly with the external pressures that could have possibly destroyed his internal equilibrium. Graced with the spirit of joyful mortification, he found that those pressures and possible destructive forces were turned into growth experiences.

Spirit of *courageous service.* Living involves doing. Through the incarnational activity of enfleshing one's mission in word and deed, St. Paul strove to realize his calling as the apostle to the Gentiles and to bring about the reconciliation which was the work of Christ. Paul's metabolism was seldom low. After rechanneling his energies beginning with the Damascus experience, he responded to God's call in building up the Kingdom of God. His activism flowed from interior prayer and self-denial. Paul's life was balanced and full.

One central dimension of Paul's apostolic work was bearing witness to the good news of Jesus Christ, God's love made visible to the world. A typical example is recorded in the Acts when Barnabas and Paul arrive at Antioch. How many times this type of sharing must have happened: "On their arrival they assembled the church and gave an account of all that God had done with them, and how he had opened the door of faith to the pagans" (Acts 14:27). In this particular instance the message and faith sharing was received with openness and joy, and they remained in Antioch for some time. More often, in attempting to fulfill the task of being an instrument of God's saving power among men, Paul was rejected and sometimes beaten (Acts 14:19; 2 Cor 11:24ff). Speaking the truth involved paying a price. But since the truth leads to freedom, the goal of the spiritual life, Paul had to speak it to remain true to his calling. He did not take the advice of the old Turkish proverb: "He that would speak the truth must have one foot in the stirrup."[8]

Missioned, being sent, seldom is limited to verbal sharing. Such was the case with St. Paul. He was commissioned to heal by living out the message he preached. Paul was a battle-scarred disciple. His concern for the poor, his gathering of money, evidence a social consciousness; his commitment to and vision of God's universal salvific will elicited extravagant energies to actualize this goal; his unwillingness to impose himself on others, thus being a burden to them, meant the retention of his tent-making profession. Sensitive to a variety of human and spiritual needs, skilled with competencies and graced with love, Paul reached out to his fellow pilgrims, helping them to grow as human beings and preparing them to experience the good news of God's mercy and love.

To live embraces loving attention, joyful mortification and courageous service. Paul is a fine model in that he followed Christ so well. Every Christian is challenged to get caught up into this way of living. The first integrating ribbon on the tail of our March kite provides solid material for homeostasis. It balances, stabilizes, as well as anchors the Christian in some depth realities. *To live* is to be one with the Spirit of Jesus and the Father; it involves a sharing in the spirit of contemplative prayer, voluntary asceticism and social concern.

Through Love: Union with the Risen Lord

The central experience of human life is being loved. So important is this experience that without it there is no hope of happiness and minimal expectation for sanity. The good news contained in the life of Jesus testifies once and for all that everyone is loved, "that our own existence in fact testifies to nothing less than our being loved by the Creator."[9] Objectively this is the case; subjectively, whether or not we come to taste the truth of God's love, this is the most significant question of our lives. St. Paul experienced God's love; what was objectively true from the first moment of his existence became subjectively a reality when he surrendered to the call of grace. Love experienced meant a rebirth which radically changed his entire existence. Throughout the rest of his life's journey and beyond, he lived *through love* in God's presence.

Though Paul knew that God's love for him was triune, it was in and through Jesus that the Father's fidelity and the Spirit's indwelling were revealed. Thus, we can focus on the quality and texture of Christ's personal love for Paul as we examine the second element in the suggested Pauline homeostatic principle. In doing this we realize that Paul knew that conversion was primarily an interior reality touching the mind and heart. His being thus transformed interiorly

showed itself in the external conversion of life-style. It is the transforming presence of Christ in our hearts and the knowledge of this
love in our understanding that brings about spiritual renewal:

> Out of his infinite glory, may he give you the power through his
> Spirit for your hidden self to grow strong, so that Christ may live in
> your hearts through faith, and then, planted in love and built on
> love, you will with all the saints have strength to grasp the breadth
> and the length, the height and depth; until, knowing the love of
> Christ, which is beyond all knowledge, you are filled with the utter
> fulness of God (Eph 3:16-19).

To live *through love* means to live in Christ Jesus: to allow his
wisdom to shape our attitudes, to surrender to his *affectivity* which
transforms our hearts, and to be enabled through his *power* to share
with others the gifts that we have received.

To live in union with the loving Lord necessarily means to be embraced by his wisdom and to share in that gift. In the book of *Wisdom*
we are told that the gift of wisdom has these traits: 1) wisdom is the
consort of God's throne; 2) to lack wisdom is to count for nothing; 3)
wisdom knows God's works; she was present when the world was
made; 4) wisdom understands what is pleasing in God's eyes; she
teaches this; 5) wisdom knows and understands everything (9:1-6,
9-11).

Insight and deep knowledge can be cold and sterile. Such is not the
case of the wisdom of Christ in which Paul shared. Rather it was a loving knowledge leading the intellect to true and full understanding.
Throughout the ages various writers have noted the relationship between love and the cognitive dimension of human knowing:

> Thus love is the parent of faith.[10]

> We could almost say he sees because he loves, and therefore loves
> although he sees.[11]

> What has to be healed in us is our true nature, made in the likeness
> of God. What we have to learn is love. The healing and the learning
> are the same thing, for at the very core of our essence we are con-
> stituted in God's likeness by our freedom, and the exercise of that
> freedom is nothing else but the exercise of disinterested love—the
> love of God for his own sake, because he is God.
>
>   The beginning of love is truth, and before he will give us his love,
> God must cleanse our souls of the lies that are in them.[12]

To live through love means that the truth given us enables us to
see and to believe. Jesus' love provides us with a vision of reality,

thereby scattering darkness and ignorance. Wisdom is to know the Father, a Father of loving fidelity and infinite mercy; our wisdom is to live from this central insight. *Through love* contains both a passive and active dimension: we are first loved in truth (passive) and then are missioned to reach out in deep concern (active). In the spiritual classic *The Cloud of Unknowing*, the importance of living and acting within God's love is stressed: "The work of love not only heals the roots of sin, but nurtures practical goodness. When it is authentic you will be sensitive to every need and respond with a generosity unspoiled by selfish intent. Anything you attempt to do without this love will certainly be imperfect, for it is sure to be marred by ulterior motives."[13]

St. Paul told the Philippians to have the same attitude that Christ had. This exhortation was grounded in lived experience, for Paul had himself put on the mind and attitudes of Christ. Paul's vision, his judgments and conception of life resembled those of Jesus who focused on the Father. In the letter to the Ephesians, Paul gives evidence of how gifted he was with God's loving wisdom when, in his letter, he describes the divine plan of salvation (1:3-14). Two verses of that magnificent passage provide sufficient witness to that wisdom: "He has let us know the mystery of his purpose, the hidden plan he so kindly made in Christ from the beginning to act upon when the times had run their course to the end; that he would bring everything together under Christ, as head, everything in the heavens and everything on earth" (vv. 9-10).

To live through love for Paul was to experience transformation of one's heart. Paul was a man deeply in love; how else explain his commitment and unmatched zeal. The love of the risen Lord touched the very center of Paul's being in an intimate and personal way, resulting in a response of deep affectivity; his heart was on fire with the concern that Jesus showed him. Several centuries after Paul, another Christian underwent a spiritual heart transplant after much struggle. This was St. Augustine. He emerged from "surgery" with the strong conviction that true life must flow from the heart: "Follow the Lord, if you will be perfect, a comrade of those among whom he speaks wisdom, who knows what to distribute to the day and to the night, so that you also may know it and so that for you lights may be in the firmament of heaven. But this will not be done unless your heart is in it."[14]

If wisdom touches our minds with truth, God's gracious love seeks to touch our hearts. Why is it that so many defense mechanisms come into play at this level? Perhaps the fear of intimacy makes us cautious: what will be demanded if I allow the Lord entrance into my life? Paradoxically we seek and need intimacy yet flee when it is offered. The conditions of intimacy—commitment, self-donation, giving up self-sufficiency—give us cause to hesitate. The tragic possibility of "having no heart" or allowing our hearts to become hard and calloused are dreadful alternatives to intimacy. Literature often speaks to this point:

> But I feel nothing, she whispered to herself. I have no heart.[15]
> Pity me that the heart is slow to learn
> What the swift mind beholds at every turn.[16]
> His sorrows will not be slight. His heart is proud and hard.[17]

Jesus came to save the whole person and all people. His love for us was integral and he sought a total response. Using the book of Deuteronomy, Jesus teaches, "and you must love the Lord your God with all your heart, with all your soul, and with all your strength" (6:4-5). Realizing in faith that God first loved us, now we are to respond in love to a God who desires our hearts. Having been gifted with love, we return that gift by loving the Father as Jesus did and by serving in the building up of the kingdom.

As God's gracious love transforms the interior of the Christian life, creating a new heart and shaping a new mind, there are external manifestations indicating a new, powerful way of life. The power of Jesus was evidenced in his love, joy, peace, in his constant patience, goodness, kindness, in his trustfulness, gentleness and self-control (Gal 5:22). Through these signs of the Spirit, the Father's love and mission were incarnated. Following the Master, Paul challenged the Galatians as well as himself to live out these values. For the sake of clarification, Paul's letter to the people of Galatia also provided concrete instances of what happens when internal renewal of heart and mind has not taken place. The "old self" of indulgence and weakness surfaces when these results are present: "fornication, gross indecency and sexual irresponsibility; idolatry and sorcery; feuds and wrangling, jealousy, bad temper and quarrels; disagreements, factions, envy; drunkenness, orgies and similar things. I warn you now, as I warned you before: those who behave like this will not inherit the kingdom of God" (5:19-21).

Using the power given him by the Father, Jesus brought about change and renewal in the lives of many. Calling Zaccheus down from the tree led an entire household to conversion. Washing the feet of the disciples taught them that to follow the Lord meant to serve. Calling Mary by name in the garden changed her depression and fear into hope and joy. The very presence of Jesus was power, transforming darkness into light, doubt into faith, apathy into love. His gaze, his tone of voice, the transparency of the Father's love were creative for anyone with the eyes of faith. When that faith was not there, Jesus experienced the pain of powerlessness and he bore that cross with much pain. Wherever growth took place, Jesus, in humility, realized that it was rooted in the Father's abiding presence and was an expression of the Father's love.

Paul lived *through love* which Christ had for him; this love power made the apostle to the Gentiles into a new man. Then, having experienced the burning power of God's call in Jesus, Paul was enabled in love to exert power in bringing others to the Father. He describes the source, purpose and strength of the Christian way of life:

> It is all God's work. It was God who reconciled us to himself through Christ and gave us the work of handing on this reconciliation. In other words, God in Christ reconciling the world to himself, not holding men's faults against them, and he has entrusted to us the news that they are reconciled. So we are ambassadors for Christ; it is as though God were appealing through us, and the appeal that we make in Christ's name is: to be reconciled to God (2 Cor 5:18-20).

To accomplish the work of the Father, power was necessary. Paul was well aware that the gifts and energies given him were not for personal gain but for others. What mattered was that all people might be in union with God, that reconciliation become a fact. The vision of faith was translated into life through the strength and courage given by the Father. Paul became an ambassador; a messenger entrusted with precious news. Through the power of proclamation and the courage of deeds, Paul shared the message of God's loving forgiveness with the people of his day, and with us who are privileged to read his letters in faith.

To live through love, then, meant for Paul a dwelling in the love of Christ Jesus. Through grace he would take on the mind and heart of the Lord as well as the power of his hands. Living through love implied an imperative: through his personal love for others, Paul must continue the process of conversion in the lives of those whom he was called to serve. The gift given, God's love and forgiveness must be passed on.

In His Presence: Union With the Father

Several years ago I was speaking with a friend about the well-being of a former classmate. His response was simple and profound: "He's all right, he lives in His presence." This type of centering provides peace and becomes the source of a "holy" life. Monica, the mother of Augustine, lived in the land of faith. Her son writes, addressing God:

> . . . and she had you as her inward teacher in the school of her heart. . . . Whosoever among them knew her greatly praised you, and honored you and loved you in her, because they recognized your presence in her heart, for the fruit of her holy life bore witness to this.[18]

C. S. Lewis, after the death of his wife, recorded an experience of presence that analogously applies to the God-human relationship:

> . . . she seems to meet me everywhere. *Meet* is far too strong a word. I don't mean anything remotely like an apparition or a voice. I don't mean even any strikingly emotional experience at any particular moment. Rather, a sort of unobtrusive but massive sense that she is, just as much as ever, a fact to be taken into account.[19]

Faith draws us to the basic fact that the Father is always with us in a variety of ways. The problem is not so much cognitive as it is experiential; through a lack of proper disposition we live outside of God's presence (this is sin at the deepest level). God is still with us but we live as though this were not the case.

In his excellent treatise *The Problem of God*, John Courtney Murray emphasizes the importance of presence:

> Over against the inconstancy and infidelity of the people, who continually absent themselves from God, the Name Yahweh affirms the constancy of God, his unchangeable fidelity to his promise of presence.[20]

> He (God) is present as the Power. Presence involves transparency; one sees through the veil of otherness into the other and knows his quality, intentions, attitudes. Thus, through his mighty works, God becomes transparent to his people. He is known to be present in faithful goodness. . . . In all his works, of judgment as of rescue, Yahweh becomes transparent, known to his people, who name him from their experience of his works.[21]

St. Paul came to experience the promise of God's dwelling with his people through grace. Then, empowered by the Spirit and healed through the power of Jesus, Paul could write to the Romans that "everyone moved by the Spirit is a son of God" and that it is this Spirit that "makes us cry out, 'Abba, Father!'" (8:14-15). Assuming the identity of a son, Paul journeyed to the Father.

The covenant theme is central throughout all of Scripture. God's word reveals the mystery of his desire to dwell with his people in a close, intimate relationship. God committed himself to be our Father, and calls us to be his people. Thus in forming a nation through Abraham, in giving the law and the prophets, in sending Jesus to reconcile, in forming a Spirit-filled Church, the Father continues to dwell in history, the God of time and space. St. Paul experienced the covenant relationship with the Father; he dwelt in the Father's tent, listening to the Father's voice and venturing forth to share that word with others.

Refusal of God's covenant is sin. Acceptance of it is grace and life. Our home is to be with God. The psalmist knew the joy of dwelling with Yahweh:

> A single day in your courts
>   is worth more than a thousand elsewhere;
> merely to stand on the steps of God's house
>   is better than living with the wicked (84:10).

Paul had spent years living out the covenant relationship. With the encounter and surrender to Christ, he gained access to the Father's dwelling. Having tasted darkness, he now knew the warmth and light of grace. To live in his presence meant life itself; anything else was death.

> But because of Christ, I have come to consider all these advantages (of the Law) as disadvantages. Not only that, but I believe that nothing can happen that will outweigh the supreme advantage of knowing Christ Jesus my Lord. For him I have accepted the loss of everything, and I look on everything as so much rubbish if only I can have Christ and be given a place in him (Phil 3:7-9).

To live in the Father's presence means necessarily to get caught up into the kingdom and the will of God. "God's kingdom is no fixed, existing order, but a living, nearing thing. Long remote, it now advances, little by little, and has come so close as to demand acceptance. Kingdom of God means a state in which God is king and consequently rules."[22] Indeed, for St. Paul the very presence of the Father within his life was synonymous with the surrender of his freedom. Decisions now were made in faith and out of love; freedom given meant freedom gained. By relating all to the furthering of the kingdom, a deep singleness of heart (purity) governed and unified the apostle's life. All was new.

The kingdom is achieved by doing the Father's will. Jesus' obedience unto death was the paradigm. Paul's highly developed sense of discernment allowed him to hear the voice of the Lord and the grace of the moment meant a response in faith. This listening and responding pattern characterized Paul's life; it meant that the Father's will was being accomplished. Paul's prayer for the Colossians indicates the centrality of God's will:

> . . . we have never failed to pray for you, and what we ask God is that through perfect wisdom and spiritual understanding you should reach the fullest knowledge of his will. So you will be able to lead the kind of life which the Lord expects of you, a life acceptable to him in all its aspects; showing the results in all good actions you do and increasing your knowledge of God (1:9-10).

Knowledge of the Father's will is no intellectual abstraction; it demands commitment and actions which are pleasing to God. This holy pragmatism stresses the dynamism of Paul's ministry and his challenge to those who follow the Lord.

To live in his presence, with the implicit willingness to promote the kingdom by doing the Father's will, means that selfishness and non-scriptural behavior are elements in opposition to the life of Christ. Yet these elements never totally disappear from life. There is that constant struggle to allow the Lord truly to be Lord of our lives; there are the perennial temptations that lead toward idolatry and wedge things and people between ourselves and the Father. Paul's life had to face these struggles; his life was one of continual conversion. His candid confession in his letter to the Romans (7:14-15) magnificently expresses the inward division of every person. Only through the grace of Christ does healing take place and only through that grace can we center on the Father's kingdom and will. Without it we flounder on stormy waters.

Life involves two essential questions: what we do and why we do what we do. This latter question deals with our motivation. Our intentions not only reveal our philosophy of life but ultimately give us our sense of identity. The Christian challenge is to center our lives on God, to serve and love for his honor and glory. Self-serving and self-preserving tendencies block purity of intention. Constantly we are invited to ever deeper levels of conversion as we strive to focus our attention on the mystery of God.

Often Paul directly called the people he served to recognize to whom all honor and glory belonged:

> Glory be to him whose power, working in us, can do infinitely more than we can ask or imagine; glory be to him from generation to generation in the Church and in Christ Jesus forever and ever. Amen (Eph 3:20-21).
>
> Glory to him who is able to give you the strength to live according to the Good News I preach, and in which I proclaim Jesus Christ, the revelation of a mystery kept secret for endless ages, but now so clear that is must be broadcast to pagans everywhere to bring them to the obedience of faith. . . . He alone is wisdom; give glory therefore to him through Jesus Christ forever and ever. Amen (Rom 16:25-27).
>
> In return, my God will fulfill all your needs, in Christ Jesus, as lavishly as only God can. Glory to God, our Father, forever and ever. Amen (Phil 4:29-30).

Honor and glory are due to God because of his majesty. The believer breaks forth in praise when God reveals himself. It is impossible to remain silent when Truth and Goodness and Beauty inundate the human spirit. Faith allows us to encounter the living and true God; our response is that of praise. Using Thomistic theology, Gabriel Braso describes well the meaning of honor and glory:

> Glory is clear knowledge together with praise of the excellence of another: *clara notitia cum laude*. Honor is the acknowledgment of this same excellence. Honor and glory, then, are acts by which our intellect recognizes an excellence existing in another being and finds it worthy of praise. Our will, on its part, accepts this superiority as a good to which it is well to tend, and, rejoicing in that good which another possesses, proclaims it and bears witness to it before others.[23]

The atmosphere in which Paul lived, namely, the loving presence of the Father, provides the springboard for his work, personal relationships and prayer. Not only did the apostle attempt to do what was good for the well-being of others, he also lived from a very specific level of intentionality; he lived for God's honor and glory. Certainly the quality of this motivation varied at times, but the ideal was ever before Paul and he strove for it with tremendous zeal and dedication. Because of this, he could write to others that they should follow his example.

Homeostasis

The spiritual life is our participation in the paschal mystery. By means of principles and guidelines we have some directions providing a perspective from which to live this life in Christ. A homeostatic principle is an internal reality giving continuity and stability to the faith life, especially when experiences of fragmentation tend to upset that life or when doubts attack the human heart stripping it of meaning and feeling. Each person is challenged to discover and cultivate a personal homeostatic principle; it may remain constant throughout life or be modified in various ways. Besides St. Paul, other believers have articulated well what possibly might be their grounding point in the Lord:

> Yesterday I had a good morning. Once again when I recollect myself, I again find the same simple demands of God: gentleness, humility, charity, interior simplicity; nothing else is asked of me. And suddenly I saw clearly why these virtues are demanded, because through them the soul becomes habitable for God and for one's neighbor in an intimate and permanent way. They make a pleasant cell of it. Hardness and pride repel, complexity disquiets. But humility and gentleness welcome, and simplicity reassures. These "passive" virtues have an eminently social character.[24]

> . . . my sole desire is that His name be praised, and that we should make every effort to serve a Lord who gives us such a reward here below. . . .[25]

> Lord, who has form'd me out of mud,
> And has redeem'd me through thy blood,
> And sanctifi'd me to do good;
>
> Purge all my sins done heretofore:
> For I confess my heavy score,
> And I will strive to sin no more.
>
> Enrich my heart, mouth, hands in me,
> With faith, with hope, with charity;
> That I may run, rise, rest with thee.[26]

Human life is lived at various levels. At times the surface of our lives can be filled with turmoil and anxieties while there is peace deep within. At other times, external forces are calm but our hearts are agitated and restless. This essay suggests that St. Paul was able to deal with the pressures, anxieties and trials of life because his life was grounded in God's life. Paul's desire was "to live through love in his presence." This homeostatic principle provided stability and continuity as he sought to "run, rise, rest" with God.

1. Hans Selye, M.D., *Stress Without Distress* (New York: J. B. Lippincott Company, 1974) 34–35.

2. C. G. Jung, *Memories, Dreams, Reflections,* recorded and edited by Aniela Jaffe, translated from the German by Richard and Clara Winston (New York: Vintage Books, 1961) 140–141.

3. Dante Alighieri, *The Divine Comedy,* trans. Lawrence Grant White (New York: Pantheon Books, 1948), canto 24, p. 171.

4. All scriptural quotations in the chapter are from *The Jerusalem Bible.*

5. Walter Kerr, *The Decline of Pleasure* (New York: Simon and Schuster, 1962) 12.

6. Gerard Manley Hopkins, "The Starlight Night."

7. ". . . and when he saw that the splendor of one of his pictures in the Exhibition dimmed his rival's that hung next to it, secretly took a brush and blackened his own" (Ralph Waldo Emerson, "Character").

8. John W. Gardner and Francesa Gardner Reese, *Know or Listen to Those Who Know* (New York: W. W. Norton & Company, Inc., 1975) 233.

9. Josef Pieper, *About Love,* trans. Richard and Clara Winston (Chicago: Franciscan Herald Press, 1972) 31.

10. John Henry Newman, "Holy Scriptures," *Essays and Sketches* (New York: Longman, Inc., 1948) 328.

11. C. S. Lewis, *A Grief Observed* (New York: The Seabury Press, 1961) 57.

12. Thomas Merton, *The Seven Storey Mountain* (New York: Harcourt, Brace and Company, 1948) 451.

13. *The Cloud of Unknowing,* ed. William Johnston (New York: Doubleday, Inc., 1973) 64.

14. *The Confessions of St. Augustine,* trans. John K. Ryan, bk. XIII, ch. 19 (New York: Image Book, 1960) 350.

15. Thornton Wilder, *The Bridge of San Luis Rey* (New York: Washington Square Press, Inc., 1955) 112.

16. Edna St. Vincent Millay, "Pity Me Not Because the Light of Day."

17. Herman Hesse, *Siddhartha,* trans. Hilda Rosner (New York: New Directions Publishing Corp., 1951).

18. *The Confessions of St. Augustine,* bk. IX, ch. 9, p. 220.

19. Lewis, *A Grief Observed* 22.

20. John Courtney Murray, *The Problem of God* (New Haven: Yale University Press, 1964) 11.

21. *Ibid.* 14–15.

22. Romano Guardini, *The Lord* (Chicago: Henry Regnery Company, 1954) 37.

23. Gabriel M. Braso, O.S.B., *Liturgy and Spirituality,* trans. Leonard J. Doyle (Collegeville, Minn.: The Liturgical Press, 1960) 59.

24. *Raïssa's Journal,* presented by Jacques Maritain (Albany, N.Y.: Magi Books, Inc., 1963) 71.

25. *The Complete Works of St. Theresa of Jesus,* trans. E. Allison Peers, II (London: Sheed and Ward, 1946) 268.

26. George Herbert, "Trinity Sunday."

10

Presence and Pedagogue
Augustine: Insights and Challenges

Along the rolling intellectual and spiritual mountain ranges of history, there stand out certain peaks more majestic and breathtaking than surrounding heights of mind and spirit. Such is the splendor and power of St. Augustine. His academic and mystical insights continue to influence not only those who have assumed an Augustinian way of life, but also those many Christians and intellectuals who are conversant with western history. The time gap of some fifteen centuries has not been able to dull or obscure either the work or the life of this man who loved so deeply his God and his fellow humans. The purpose of this chapter is to demonstrate that Augustine's insights into human existence are valid for contemporary times and further, that these insights implicitly present some very forceful and extremely clear challenges to all of us.

Augustine's Spirit of Christian Friendship

One of the greatest needs of the human heart is the need to belong, to be a part of a larger whole. Individualism, so rampant in our century, fails to bring the radical happiness desired by every person. In fact, the ultimate term of individualism is loneliness. People need people. Augustine emphasized the value of friendship and community, not only in his writings but also in his life. He gathered around him people with similar visions, values and life-styles. In the following description of friendship, which can be easily telescoped into embracing the larger concept of community, we find a perspective of intimacy at once profound and inspirational:

When we are oppressed by poverty, when mourning makes us sad or bodily pain makes us restless, when exile dejects us or any evil whatever afflicts us, then there are good people who not only understand the art of rejoicing with those who rejoice, but also of weeping with those who weep; people who know how to speak a cheerful word and how to hold a conversation that does us good. In this way much that is bitter is softened, much that weights us down is lightened, so many failures are overcome. But it is really God who does this, through and in people. On the other hand, when we are swimming in riches, when we are free of sadness and enjoy good bodily health, while living in a free country, but having to live together with people among whom there is not even one in whom we can place trust, not even one from whom we need not be in dread and fear of guilt, deceit, hate, discord, or falsity, then do not all the other things of life become hard and bitter, and lose all joy and color? Whenever a man is without a friend, not a single thing in the world appears friendly to him.[1]

The insight challenges us to several responses.

To grow humanly so as to become capable of deep friendship. Growth is not automatic. The proper nutrients must be present, certain obstacles avoided. Augustine would certainly challenge us to be familiar with the principles of human growth and development, seeing these as necessary building blocks to a full spiritual life. In this area of growth, professional help may at times be needed; more often, perhaps, simple discipline stimulating the dormancy of our minds and hearts.

To develop the art of conversation and a sense of compassion. Much conversation tends toward the negative; much is monological and empty. What a joy to find a dialogical person, someone who knows how to listen from the heart and respond appropriately. Friendship and community are utterly impossible without healthy communication (especially the non-verbal type). Hopefully, we are all aware of the power of words. Pascal is credited with the following statement: "Cold words freeze people, and hot words scorch them, and bitter words make them bitter and wrathful words make them wrathful. Kind words also produce their own image on men's souls; and a beautiful image it is. They smooth and quiet and comfort the hearer."[2] Commpassionate people are builders of community. Feeling the joy of others, they participate in the celebration; sensing human anguish caused by loss, they share the burden. One function of friendship and community is precisely this: to share success *and* failure, to weep *and* rejoice together, to accept each other totally and unconditionally. These realities are grounded in the Trinity, the wellspring of Augustine's theology and reflections. Our model is Jesus: "As the Father has loved me, so I have loved you. . . . love one another, as I have loved you" (John 15:9, 12).[3]

To risk and entrust ourselves to others in prudence. Reaching out is a risky business. One is off balance and vulnerable in such a gesture. The shelled turtle has mobile security, but to enjoy the sun, wind and rain it must come out. Once out, it will have to face various dangers and risks. Such is life! To choose life means to risk getting hurt. In entering a friendship one becomes responsible, whole, but also vulnerable. A note of caution may not be out of place. Since entrusting ourselves to others gives them considerable power over our lives, this should be done with prudence.

Augustine's Spirit of Sharing Faith

The core of Christian faith is a personal relationship with Jesus Christ. Through Christ, the Christian goes to the Father. Gifted with their Spirit, he is enabled to call God "Abba" and is drawn deeply into the trinitarian life. Augustine was a man of faith; his identity was derived from this gratuitous reality. Because he knew the Lord Jesus, Augustine sought to express this central dimension not merely theologically, but experientially as well. His autobiography, the *Confessions*, is essentially a faith-sharing event. From this work a single example is selected because of its profundity and rich intimacy. Shortly before the death of his mother Monica, she and her newly converted son underwent a mystical experience. Augustine describes it:

> . . . [Monica] and I stood alone leaning in a window which looked inwards to the garden within the house where we were staying, at Ostia on the Tiber; for there we were away from everybody, resting for the sea-voyage from the weariness of our long journey by land. There we talked together, she and I alone, in deep joy; and *forgetting the things that were behind and looking forward to those that were before,* we were discussing in the presence of Truth, which You are, what the eternal life of the saints could be like, *which eye has not seen nor ear heard, nor has it entered into the heart of man.* But with the mouth of our heart we panted for the high waters of Your fountain, the fountain of life which is with You: that being sprinkled from that fountain according to our capacity, we might in some sense meditate upon so great a matter.[4]

This shared historical event is a call to all of us.

To share experiences of faith with each other. Not only is this important in terms of personal confirmation of how the Lord is working in our lives, but it can also be a strong stimulus and inspiration to the faith-life of others. A marriage cannot grow unless husband and wife share their daily experiences; Christians who do not share their faith (beyond the "public" sharing of liturgy) endanger its development. God calls us to share the gifts he has given us. One of the greatest gifts is faith.

To center our lives on the Lord. In *The Divine Comedy,* Dante describes how, with the help of his faithful guide Virgil, he was able to pass through a sheet of fire on his journey heavenward. It was only by gazing through the fire in the direction of his beloved Beatrice that Dante could endure the immediate obstacle and suffering. We must ask ourselves what or who is the center of our life; where is our focus. Monica and Augustine centered on God and in this we perceive a radical simplicity in their lives. Absent is that sense of restlessness and agitation resulting from a fragmented and hurried life. With such a faith-centering we can better appreciate the meaning of the term "realized eschatology."

To make explicit what is implicit. Interior realities seek expression like a volcano releasing its pressure-filled energies. The interior reality of faith expresses itself in witness. The cartoon depicting two clams on the beach, one saying to the other, "I can't clam up; I've got a pearl inside of me the size of which you won't believe," exemplifies the point. Goodness and love are diffusive. Faith is a love relationship between God and humans. Anyone alive with this reality will appropriately share it with others; in that sharing both parties grow.

Augustine's Spirit of Learning

C. S. Lewis wrote in his autobiography, "A young man who wishes to remain a sound atheist cannot be too careful of his reading."[5] Reading, study and reflection are nutrients not only for our minds but for our hearts and life-styles as well. Sweet corn soaked in salt water before roasting is saturated with moisture and the taste of salt. Likewise, a person's mind is deeply influenced and shaped by the experiences and beliefs exposed to it. Augustine was a brilliant scholar. Although at times wandering down metaphysically erroneous paths, his mind searched out the truth at every moment. One of the great Roman poets, Cicero, became an instrument through which God touched the depths of Augustine's soul:

That particular book is called *Hortensius* and contains an exhortation to philosophy. Quite definitely it changed the direction of my mind, altered my prayers to you, O Lord, and gave me a new purpose and ambition. Suddenly all the vanity I had hoped in I saw as worthless, and with an incredible intensity of desire I longed after immortal wisdom. I had begun that journey which was to lead to you.[6]

In an age when intellectual institutions are prolific, Augustine offers us several challenges.

To appreciate the value of education and the significance of the learning process. Anything which becomes universal tends to depreciate in value. Education, at least in our country, is something not only universal but mandatory. This fact must not allow us to falter in our love and pursuit of truth. Delving deeply into the mysteries of realities in search of wisdom must be our constant task. What Cardinal Newman sensed in his day must be shunned: "In the present day mistiness is the mother of wisdom."[7] Clarity of vision and growth in faith underlie Augustine's hunger for the truth.

To discern internally and externally the anti-intellectual trends of our time. Coming from an educational tradition that has overemphasized the cognitive domain of learning, an imbalanced overreaction now focuses on the affective and behavioral realms. All three domains are important and must be given proper attention. While educating our emotions and deepening our concern for life-styles, we must also protect, as a wellspring, the intellectual source of the heart and hands. It is still reason under faith that directs our lives.

To continue to update ourselves professionally and theologically. The explosion of knowledge has been astounding. No one can or should attempt to read everything. The danger, in the face of such a quantity of material, is to fail to develop a principle of selection and exclusion. Augustine would demand that we continually grow in our ideas and attitudes. There can be no excuse (e.g. "I have no time") for not being competent in our specific vocation nor being ignorant about the general state of our world. Needless to say, priority must be given to our growing knowledge of God.

Augustine's Spirit of Human Sacredness

The psalmist speaks of the dignity of the human person:

Ah, what is man that you should spare a thought for him,
the son of man that you should care for him?
Yet you have made him little less than a god,
you have crowned him with glory and splendor. . . (8:4-5).

Shakespeare approaches the human person from yet a different perspective, pointing out the pride that can govern life:

> . . . But man, proud man,
> Dress'd in a little brief authority,
> Most ignorant of what he's most assured—
> His glassy essence,—like an angry ape,
> Plays such fantastic tricks before high heaven
> As make the angels weep.[8]

Augustine experienced the paradoxes of life. Despite sin, he maintained an extraordinary reverence for the human person. An acquired reverence both for others and himself eventually led him to a faith vision from which he saw the nobility of the person:

> I confess it, I give myself easily to the love of friends and I rest in it without cares, especially when I am tired of the vexations of this world. For I feel that God is there, and in safety I give myself up to him and safely I rest. In this security of love I no longer fear the insecurity of tomorrow, the insecurity of human frailty about which I complained earlier. . . . The ideas and thoughts I entrust to a faithful friend who is filled with Christian *caritas*, I entrust no longer to a man, but to God, because the man remains in God and is faithful through him.[9]

A desperate humanism marks our times. The human person is put at the center of everything and continually finds this mislocation too heavy a weight to carry. Augustine challenges us to see every human as a relational being, gaining identity from the center of existence— the Lord God. In this context we come to a true humanism. Thus there are challenges.

Truly to see the sacredness of others and the mystery of God's indwelling. The Gospel of St. John is terribly clear: "Through [the Word] all things came to be, not one thing had its being but through him" (John 1:3). The human person is a creature, the handiwork of God. So intimate is this relationship of creator-creature that wherever there is disrespect shown for any creature, that disrespect redounds to the Father. As creatures we live and move and have our being only because of God's gift of existence. Thus, we are sacred beings! Because God is present within and among us, we have a dignity beyond description. Were this realized, how different the world would be!

To come to a healthy self-concept based on our being fashioned in God's image and likeness. Modern psychology has emphatically demonstrated that many human beings do not hold themselves in proper esteem. Inferiority complexes, enslavement by fears[10] and neurotic guilts have caused self-hatred leading to discouragement, despair and suicide. Augustine, though struggling often through the dark valley of self-doubt, came to experience himself loved by God. In this personal knowledge of the good news he came to see himself as lovable; this in turn freed him to see the true worth of others. In spite of personal and collective sin, Augustine was convinced in faith that the Father's love and forgiveness conquered sin and death. He would have all strive to be open to this love and to come to the joy of knowing our true identity as beloved children of God.

Prayerfully to strive to put on the mind and heart of Christ. St. Paul, admired deeply by Augustine, tells of his own sacredness in terms of his relationship with the Lord:

> In other words, through the Law I am dead to the Law, so that now I can live for God. I have been crucified with Christ, and I live now not with my own life but with the life of Christ who lives in me. The life I now live in this body I live in faith: faith in the Son of God who loved me and who sacrificed himself for my sake (Gal 2:19-20).

This type of seeing and feeling has graced all the saints throughout the history of the Church. Augustine in a profound way passed through this transformation and has shared it with the world through his writings. There is consolation in knowing that all of this is a life-long task, that conversion is always an ongoing process. Never in this life will the necessity of growing cease. We become more and more human as we participate in the mind and heart and work of the risen Lord. In coming to appreciate the dignity of the human person, Augustine probably experienced what Emerson later put into words: "A new person is to me a great event and hinders me from sleep."[11]

Augustine's Spirit of Scriptural Formation

Is it true that the home, school and church no longer are the major formative factors in shaping human values? Have television, movies and magazines aggressively, and perhaps without too much opposition, gained ascendancy in influencing the culture and personal lives of all of us? Augustine had to deal with the whole problem of value formation, though the opposition to Christian values did not come from the mass media as we understand it today. The negative forces were of a different nature but no less formidable. His own mind was affected by the pagan culture, and, even after coming into contact with God's word, he was unable to understand what the Scriptures really meant because of an "obtuse spirit."[12] By grace, Augustine was able to receive the Spirit of understanding and from that point on, Scripture became one of the most significant forces shaping his thought and life. Realizing what a blessing God's word was, he urged others to taste and see the goodness of the Lord in revelation:

> We act in this fashion; we read with our brothers who come to us weary from the turmoil of the world, asking in our company rest in the Word of God, in prayers, in hymns and spiritual canticles; we converse with them, console and exhort them, and build up in them whatever we notice is needed for their progress.[13]

Like the prophet Isaiah,[14] Augustine invites us to come before God with attentive listening.

To allow our lives to be shaped by God's word. Revelation is another aspect of God's love. This unfolding of his fidelity and covenant elicits from our hearts, if they are in any way sensitive, a profound response of praise and thanksgiving. For it is in God's word that the mystery of the divine plan and the warm invitation to cooperate in its accomplishment are unveiled. It is in God's word that we come to know who we are and who he is. If we live in fear and ignorance, if we continually worry and allow anxieties to govern our lives, if we fret about the future and wallow in the past, does this not mean that we have failed to allow Scripture to permeate our lives? It would be sadly revealing, perhaps, to evaluate honestly the amount of time and energy we expend in exposing our minds and hearts to the mass media as compared to that used to expose them to God's word. No wonder then that our values are twisted and our hearts are malformed. If the clay refuses to be shaped by the potter, it remains its unformed self.

To understand that Scripture is a primary source for religious experience.[15] It was in a garden that Augustine turned to the word of God in St. Paul's letter to the Romans. The long process of conversion was reaching its climax when, in the context of God's word, Augustine underwent a profound interior change. That moment offered Augustine the clarity he needed to respond to the call of the Father. The Scriptures present to us the mysteries of our faith; what happens in God's word is supposed to happen *now* in our lives. The annunciation account is not simply an historical event; what happened to Mary is to happen in our lives as well. We are to hear God's word, allow it to enter our lives, and then, responding to that word, bear fruit in good deeds. The incarnation is an ongoing reality and happens today. Scripture often draws us into the experience of these mysteries.

To translate the gospel into action. Nothing is perhaps more difficult than living out the truth that has been given us in Christ. The message and the action are one and the same: love. Indeed, it is not terribly difficult to know the message; the problem is in implementation, ". . . for men are most anxious to find truth but very reluctant to accept it. . . . In short, finding out truth is not so hard; what is hard is not to run away from truth once we have found it."[16] Augustine was driven toward authenticity. What he knew and felt he strove to live. Though failures were many, his life presents a challenging model of wholeness. Walter Nigg writes of that process in which Augustine sought to unify prayer and life:

> In his new existence he came face to face with the problem to which there is no final solution—that of putting the gospel into actual practice. It is a problem that can be solved only by a great spiritual effort and a readiness to commit oneself. With his new clarity of vision, Augustine realized that his most vital task was to apply his religion to his daily life.[17]

Augustine's Spirit of Internalization

In St. Mark's Gospel, Jesus deals sternly with the Pharisees:

> How accurately Isaiah prophesied about you hypocrites when he wrote, "This people pays me lip service but their heart is far from me. Empty is the reverence they do me because they teach as dogmas mere human precepts." . . . Nothing that enters a man from outside can make him impure; that which comes out of him, and only that, constitutes impurity (7:6-7, 15).

Our Lord was primarily concerned with the insideness of our lives. Augustine likewise realized that the deeper recesses of life were what mattered the most. An example of the primacy of interiority comes from Augustine's rule:

> And do not say that you have a pure soul if you have an impure eye, because the unchaste eye is the sign of an unchaste soul. And when unchaste souls speak in mutual gazes without any words being spoken and take delight in their passion for each other, then chastity flees from their souls even though their bodies are not defiled by unclean actions.[18]

This inward journey is the core of human and divine life. Dante mapped his travels in *The Divine Comedy*, Teresa of Avila recorded the many levels of interiority in her *Interior Castle*, Augustine invites us into his inner sanctuary in his *Confessions*. The journey is still being made in our time. A literary genius of our own times records this discourse with a child:

> "I saw [God]. I did so," said the child.
>
> "We will go and look all about," I comforted, "for that is good to do. But mostly we will look inside, for that is where we ache and where we laugh and where at last we die. I think it is most there that He is very close."[19]

Augustine's voice challenges us even today.

To strive to live authentic lives. One of the consequences of sin is undoubtedly a fragmentation of life. We are no longer whole! Many of our words and deeds issue from the periphery of our being. Healing is needed on every level: physical, psychological, social and spiritual. Integrity seems so rare and episodic. Ibsen's dialogue sadly states:

> Relling: He is suffering from an acute attack of integrity.
> Gina: Integrity?
> Hedvig: Is that a kind of disease?
> Relling: Yes, it's a national disease, but it only appears sporadically.[20]

Authenticity results from the internalization of values. We must appropriate that which is true, good and beautiful. The process is at once simple and difficult. In response to the question of how we make something our own, an eighth grade boy responded: "Well, when you love something so much that it gets down in your heart and gets stuck there and can't get out, then it's your own!" A budding Plato, indeed!

To avoid legalism and formalism. Father Vincent Dwyer in his *Genesis II* program tells how the abbot of the monastery used to warn the monks: "We can do holy things all day without becoming holy!" Strange to say, the human spirit is capable of living with simple compliance to a law, deriving from this some type of satisfaction and security ("at least I did it"). This type of conduct can ultimately be very empty and vain; it can consistently be a sham or hoax. St. Paul vehemently attacks this approach because of its spiritlessness, for law without the spirit is deadly. We are daily challenged to ferret out the areas of gross legalism invading our lives.

To take seriously our interior tendencies. Even from a cursory reading of the *Confessions*, one quickly realizes that Augustine was in touch with the inner movements of his spirit, both those which were healthy, thus of God, and those which led him away from his Source. He was also keenly aware of the complexity of these inner movements and the difficulty of true discernment. "Man's hairs are easier to count than his affections and the movements of his heart."[21] Despite this challenging task, Augustine was willing, without excessive introspection, to attempt to discern how God was working within him and to evaluate the quality of his response.[22] This same interiority is part of our lives. We tend to play down interior urges, not to take them seriously. We drift on the surface and allow the sensate culture to dominate our life. Only in moments of tragedy or great wonder are we shocked back to the more interior dimensions of our spirit. Augustine lived intensely; he knew that the Father was always working. Our challenge is similar: "to live through love in his presence" (Eph 1:4).

Spirituality for Today

Every age has a need for sages. The journey of life becomes less difficult, indeed even joyful, when we are accompanied by wise guides who offer deep insights along the way and who are not unwilling to challenge us to a fuller life. Such a guide is St. Augustine. What a privilege we have as a Church to have in our treasury the maps and directions of this dedicated and scholarly servant of God. Summarizing this chapter in an anachronistic manner, we might imagine Augustine offering an M.A. in spirituality at the University of Hippo. In a three-year summer school program with Augustine as teacher the catalogue might look like this:

M.A. in Christian Spirituality

Th 101 *Christian Friendship*
The significance of friendship; human growth and development; the art of conversation; a philosophy of trust and prudence.

Th 102 *Faith Sharing*
The meaning of faith in terms of personal relationship with Christ; experiential seminar on sharing faith; the concept of centering and contemplation; the art of articulation.

Ed 201 *Philosophy of Learning*
The value of education; methodologies of knowledge; intellectual and anti-intellectual trends today; processes of continuing education.

Ps 202 *The Sacred and the Profane*
Human sacredness; understanding our real self; self-images and culture; the role of prayer in viewing self and others.

RS 301 *Scripture*
The principles underlying Scripture; elements that shape our lives; meaning of religious experience; process of doing the truth.

Ps 302 *Internalization and Value Processing*
The question of appropriation; meaning of authenticity and integrity; obstacles to internalization; discernment of spirits.

Once degreed, the graduate would perhaps find added meaning in Augustine's prayer:

> Late have I loved Thee, O Beauty, so ancient and so new; late have I loved Thee! For behold Thou wert within me, and I outside; and I sought Thee outside and in my unloveliness fell upon those lovely things that Thou hast made. Thou wert with me and I was not with Thee. I was kept from Thee by those things, yet had they not been in Thee, they would not have been at all. Thou didst call and cry to me and break open my deafness: and Thou didst send forth Thy beams and shine upon me and chase away my blindness: Thou didst breathe fragrance upon me, and I drew in my breath and do now pant for Thee: I tasted Thee, and now hunger and thirst for Thee: Thou didst touch me, and I have burned for Thy peace.[23]

1. T. J. Van Bavel, "The Evangelical Inspiration of the Rule of St. Augustine," *The Downside Review* (September 1975).

2. Cited in *Bits and Pieces* (Fairfield, N.J.: Economics Press, Inc., 1976).

3. All Scripture quotations in this chapter are from *The Jerusalem Bible*.

4. *The Confessions of St. Augustine*, trans. F. J. Sheed, bk. IX, ch. 10 (New York: Sheed & Ward, 1943) 199–200.

5. C. S. Lewis, *Surprised by Joy: The Shape of My Early Life* (New York: Harcourt, Brace & World, Inc., 1955) 191.

6. *Confessions*, bk. III, ch. 4, p. 45.

7. John Henry Newman, "Prospects of the Anglican Church," *Essays and Sketches* (New York: Longman, Green & Co., 1948) 368.

8. *Measure for Measure*, Act II, sc. 2.

9. From a book translated, compiled and edited by Robert E. Heslinga, O.S.A., Epistula 73, *One Mind, One Heart: Augustinian Spirituality of the Religious Life*, 1973.

10. The range of fears is great. In *Bits and Pieces* (May 1976) the following statement appears: "Psychologists now list—and have names for—700 phobias. No one, apparently, is immune, everyone fearing something. They range from Arachibutyrophobia, the fear of getting peanut butter stuck to the roof of the mouth, to Phobophobia, the fear of fear."

11. Ralph Waldo Emerson, *Friendship* (New York: Heritage Press, 1941) 67.

12. The early books of the *Confessions* describe well that without the proper mental disposition the Scriptures remain essentially inscrutable.

13. Source unknown.

14. "Oh, come to the water all you who are thirsty; . . . Listen, listen to me, and you will have good things to eat and rich food to enjoy. Pay attention, come to me; listen, and your soul will live" (Isa 55:1–3).

15. David M. Stanley, "Introduction: Scripture as a Normative Guide to Religious Experience," *A Modern Scriptural Approach to the Spiritual Exercises* (St. Louis: The Institute of Jesuit Sources, 1973) 1–14.

16. Gerald Vann, O.P., *Saint Thomas Aquinas* (Chicago: Benziger Brothers, 1940) 76.

17. Walter Nigg, *Warriors of God*, ed. and trans. Mary Ilford (New York: Alfred A. Knopf, 1972) 106.

18. Julian C. Resch, O. Praem., *The Rule of St. Augustine*, ch. 6 (De Pere, Wis.: St. Norbert Abbey Press).

19. Loren Eiseley, *The Night Country* (New York: Charles Scribner's Sons, 1973) 76.

20. *The Wild Duck*, Act III, *The Best Known Works of Ibsen* (New York: The Book League of America, 1941) 309.

21. *Confessions*, bk. IV, ch. 14, p. 75.

22. A method of how to do this is described by George A. Aschenbrenner, S.J., in "Consciousness Examen," *Review for Religious* 31, no. 1 (January 1972).

23. *Confessions*, bk. X, ch. 27, p. 236.

11

Presence and Potpourri
The Ho-Ho, Hum-Hum Principle

Simplicity is a quality that is rapidly gaining new admirers in our world of complexity and confusion. An innate urge arises deep within the human spirit for a limited number of truths and principles by which life might be guided and lived. Socrates offered the principle that an "unexamined life is not worth living"; we read in the *Little Prince* that what is essential in life is invisible to the eye; Jonathan Livingston Seagull suggests that perfection and excellence are core values by which the mystery of existence might be well spent; even the entertainment world has an implicit, simplistic philosophy in the crooner's "I did it my way!" How quickly our need for simplicity finds waiting vendors!

Claiming a vendor's right, I offer for sale yet another principle as a source of decisions and actions. Observing four perennially pernicious enemies of humanity, i.e., discouragement, hostility, dishonesty and over-seriousness, my proposed principle is that *all* one has to do in life is gently hum and diligently live the "ho-ho, hum-hum" principle. More explicitly, as the virtues of *hope-ho*spitality, *humility-humo*r are cultivated, the four enemies of life are increasingly warded off with the result that peace and happiness, qualities desired by all, have a greater possiblity of being realized.

Discouragement vs. Hope

William Gibson's *Miracle Worker* presents an intriguing dialogue between James Keller, the atheistic and arrogant brother of Helen

Keller, and Annie Sullivan, Helen's teacher. James makes the apodictic statement that eventually everyone gives up; it is simply a matter of time. Annie's concise but profound reply is, "Maybe you all do. It's my idea of the original sin." Giving up, one of the common forms of discouragement, is widely practiced in our times. It symbolizes the "downness" so rampant in a century satiated by anxiety and depersonalization. Indescribable suffering, years of mental anguish, torturous crosses borne in silence force many people toward discouragement and even despair.

Discouragement has always found expression in the literary forum. Dante's famous inscription etched on the gate leading into hell has at times been transposed over the portals of the lives of many an individual: "Abandon hope, all you who enter here." Just as discouraging is the observation made of the hired man by Robert Frost in "The Death of a Hired Man":

> Nothing to look backward to with pride,
> nothing to look forward to with hope.

Despite the hidden origins of such feelings, everyone knows that discouragement, despair and depression blind and distort; they arrogantly obstruct the full view of reality; they insidiously isolate, divide and ultimately destroy. There are no automatic exemptions here, no lobbyists strong enough to remove such an enemy. Everyone is vulnerable to discouragement.

The ancient Greeks credited the proud and mighty Prometheus with instilling in people the gift of hope. The Christian attributes this gift to God: "May the God of hope bring you such peace and joy in your faith that the strength of the Holy Spirit will remove all bounds to hope" (Rom 15:13). The prodigious power of hope lies in its ability to shape one's life. Various qualities of hope tell of its pristine beauty.

Hope elicits a healthy expectation. The hopeful person ventures into the future with the certitude that change, growth and happiness are real possibilities. In terms of human development, there is essentially no shortage of sufficient resources but only a problem of proper utilization of the marvelous energies stockpiled in the human heart and mind. Obviously, hope's expectation goes far beyond the human domain, for its deepest recesses reside in the realm of spirituality. Humanism as such allows for no ultimate hope; God is both the primary source of expectation and its object. Nor should we forget that hope is always grounded in an expectant faith.

Hope is born of trust. The person of hope must be one who has the ability to trust; risking all when security is so inviting; plunging, like Abraham, into the unknown future; saying yes, like Mary, before consequences are carefully spelled out. We find in the confidence of Abraham and the trust of Mary wealthy tomes of hope reserved in the libraries of our tradition, perhaps too seldom withdrawn by twentieth-century humans for reverent scrutiny. Trust is the subjective disposition allowing the reality of hope to find a home. Remove trust, and then hope—like King Lear—cast forth from its legitimate and necessary milieu, wanders aimlessly amid the turbulent, hostile elements. Hope's survival is unlikely if not impossible without a radical confidence.

The heart of hope is promise. Some promise a rose garden, others a rainbow, still others the moon. The Christian promise is the presence of the Lord. "And know that I am with you forever, yes, even to the end of time" (Matt 28:20). Christian hope is presence. Emerson once wrote that "we judge a man's wisdom by his hope." Wise indeed are those who put all their hope and trust in the Lord. This promise of presence, springing from God's word, transcends the sincere but fragile promises of humans. From one perspective Christian hope is already realized: Christ is truly with us. Yet, because of sin, blindness and fear, this hope of promised presence is always in process. The intrinsic incompleteness of hope (its "not yet" quality) demands the diligent fostering of this virtue.

The religious especially should be a sign of joyful hope to the world. To say this does not exclude from life the moments, weeks, even years of doubt and agonizing discouragement. However, if discouragement verging on despair is a way of life, a radical disposition, one would have to question the very existence of faith, the *sine qua non* of hope. A central aspect of religious life is the Trinitarian structure of a faith leading to hope which in turn overflows into love and service.

In spite of the fact that example is much more effective than advice, three suggestions for the cultivation of hope are proposed:

1) A religious should foster an abiding consciousness of the promise made. A good memory is imperative to hope, and fidelity is the marriage partner of memory, a fidelity to the person of Christ. Forgetting leads to infidelity; in fact, it is a necessary prerequisite. Daily prayer and lived liturgies keep the promise alive and bring it to fruition. God is with us: Father, Son and Spirit! The discourtesy of forget-

ting about this indwelling not only tells of insensitivity but quickly leads to hopelessness.

2) A religious should expect nobility and goodness within community as well as outside it. Though at times disappointed in unrealized expectations, the hopeful person will frequently discover how good people really are. The treasured qualities of goodness and magnanimity, though often hidden in shyness, concealed in humility or passed over in inadvertent hurry, need a tender response. Great expectations from God, from others and from oneself make life exciting and hopeful. Living with people of expectation turns life into an adventure and a challenge. Without expectation community life is neither vital nor viable.

3) A religious should see discipline and perseverance as pillars of hope. A firm though human discipline of mind, choice and affections as well as a principled perseverance in spite of childish pettiness, unjust treatment or lack of personal understanding will be a model to the world that, in at least one segment of contemporary history, hope is built on firm foundations. An undisciplined hope is like a marriage without fidelity; it is a sham! A hope-filled religious has the cultivated discernment to say an evangelical "yes" or "no" and weather both loneliness and rejection.

The tug of war played by discouragement and hope is no game. Human lives are at stake. Our age is in desperate need of paradigms of hope. Contemporary men and women have a right to expect to find such models within the Church. Historically, religious communities have been fountainheads of this virtue. God's promised help makes this possible: "And truly everything that was written long ago in the scriptures was meant to teach us something about hope from the examples scripture gives of how people who did not give up were helped by God" (Rom 15:4).

Hostility vs. Hospitality

Human existence is a fragile structure. Like glassware perched on narrow shelving, so vulnerable to even slight though unintended jars, individual and communal life is subject to being broken and shattered by various forces of hostility. There is no need to speak of the destruction wrought by warfare and straw-dog mayhem; more subtle and less easily detected are the forms of hostility born of a stare, cold silence, apathy, gossip and negativism. Because these hostile elements violate no civil code and involve no visible sanctions, there is a strange acceptance and unconscious internalization of such dehumanizing attitudes and actions.

The attitude of hostility basically positions "the other" as enemy. The posture of hostility fluctuates between attack and defense. If the other appears weak then attack is the order of the day. The offensive is launched not only at ideas but at persons as well. More subtle is a second unprincipled position of hostility: defensiveness. Walls arise; a supposed inferiority conveniently provides isolation; a psychological retreat distances one from the other. A defensive person has a surprisingly high level of hostility. Regardless of the posture of hostility, it would take an eloquent and sophistic lawyer to defend the innocence of a "hostile Christian."

As hope counteracts a person's tendency to become discouraged, so hospitality is a partial cure for hostility. God's word is very direct in stressing the virtue of hospitality:

> "If any of the saints are in need you must share with all of them and you should make hospitality your special concern" (Rom 12:13).
>
> "Continue to love each other like brothers, and always remember to welcome strangers . . ." (Heb 13:1-2).
>
> "Welcome each other into your homes without grumbling" (1 Pet 4:9).

The warm, personal welcome graciously extended to the stranger leaves one awed. For is not the stranger someone to be feared as potentially dangerous? Is not the modern spirit primarily selective and exclusive as to whom it admits into one's world? Unusual indeed is this Christian ideal which welcomes everyone as if the world contained no strangers, as if their home were planet-wide and had no boundaries! Yet this is not extraordinary if the Christian God is a God of universal and radical hospitality.

Hospitality is a spring enriching life. It is the gateway to friendship and love. It is the fulfillment of the gospel and realized homecoming. It is a duty and a privilege, longed for when absent, supportive when experienced. It is filled with dangers and bruises, tears and joys. It is the smile of acceptance and the warm tone of affirmation. Far from the superficial hospitality of the annual Christmas party, sincere hospitality cannot be turned on and off. The fact that some people have no relational home because they are unwelcomed by others and unable, tragically, to be hospitable even to themselves, hints at a common and unhealthy situation. Thus there is a constant need to foster hospitality.

The thesis that one of the genuine hallmarks of religious life is a warm and affable hospitality which welcomes the stranger is more than theory and thus must find expression in practice. It is in concrete, specific, definite words and deeds that hospitality is incarnated. Some hospitable suggestions:

1) Take the initiative! Natural shyness is an easy excuse leading to a lack of introductions and challenging invitations. Yet human courtesy, to say nothing of simple Christian graciousness, demands that we welcome kindly into the group any new arrival. Taking the first step can be difficult and even embarrassing; yet it can also be very rewarding and surprisingly pleasant. At the core of initiative is the poignant perception of a need—the need to belong—and it is not left unfulfilled by a hospitable person.

2) Ask revelatory questions! While respecting the right to privacy and employing common sense, a key sign of hospitality is a sincere interest in the world of the "stranger." Questions which gently probe the other's thoughts, works, interests and opinions have a tendency to foster feelings of being accepted and important. A delicate balance is needed here. Ungracious probing or undisciplined questioning can lead to hostility. This suggestion of asking revelatory questions obviously applies to old as well as new acquaintances. If such questions are not asked it may well happen that even those we once considered friends drift off to distant lands and become strangers, though sharing the same table and work.

3) Have a fireplace! It is possible that the graciously welcomed stranger eventually and sadly discovers that the apparently welcoming world (be it person or community) has no fireplace, i.e., no real warmth or tenderness. These qualities, together with intimacy, trust and respect, are the core of Christian hospitality. Coldness of heart, prejudicial thought and impositions on the good will of others are forces that extinguish the flame of Christian openness.

In the recesses of the human spirit the forces of hostility and hospitality vie for ascendancy. Honest anxiety arises in the realization that in subtle undetected ways hostility can break through to do its damage in the life around us. Only a vigilant spirit can unequivocally squelch such moments of dehumanization; only a sensitive and generous spirit can affirm and welcome another into its home.

Dishonesty vs. Humility

Discouragement and hostility are joined by a third even more deadly enemy of God and humans: dishonesty. Dishonesty makes sight unreliable, sound unreal and reality undiscoverable. Living in the land of falsity and untruth, dwelling in the caverns of deception and lies, wallowing in the winter of half-truths and vague statements, the human spirit dies a slow, painful, inevitable death. Bold dishonesty blatantly paints black into white, negative into positive, falsity into truth; mild dishonesty writes out of context and speaks with hidden assumptions.

The real tragedy surrounding dishonesty is that a realistic solution is almost impossible since it must necessarily involve a willingness to live in the light of truth. As long as alcoholics deny their enslavement to the bottle, they remain practicing alcoholics; as long as drug addicts claim to have no need of the stuff, they remain users; as long as sinners are unwilling to face the fact of a broken covenant, they remain in sin. Dishonesty is its own best friend, for it will survive as long as it is persistently denied.

Of constant urgency, therefore, is the necessity of grounding one's life in the truth. Striving to know and acknowledge God, oneself, others and the whole of history calls for diligence, creativity and the ability to face facts. Christian tradition has always held that it is the virtue of humility which roots our life in truth. To live outside humility is to live in darkness and unreality. In *The Interior Castle* St. Teresa of Avila writes that "there is nothing that matters so much to us as humility," and again, "humility, humility—the Lord allows himself to be vanquished by this virtue."

Because it is truth, humility makes possible the birth of justice and peace. The present political turmoil in our own country stems directly from a lack of credibility. Extreme cases of injustice and violent social unrest have been the tragic consequences. Once truth is abandoned for whatever reason, poisonous ramifications spread throughout the network of human existence. The Christian's task is to search out the truth and to live within its boundaries. Humility leads to a land of light instead of darkness, a kingdom of freedom instead of slavery.

Humility, like the virtues of hope and hospitality, is essentially a gift. This fact does not exempt anyone from the obligation of disposing oneself to receive this gift by cultivating an atmosphere of openness. Three suggestions:

1) Seriously reflect on the words contained in the Epistle of St. James, 1:19-25. The "mirror, mirror on the wall" test has amazing results.

2) Practice a specific form of bodily mortification. The proportionality between temperance and perception of truth is incredibly close. Mortification abets temperance, which in turn abates deception.

3) Renew or deepen one's appreciation of the sacrament of reconciliation. Being essentially a sacrament of humility, it aids in the discovery of the full truth of our lives. A rather personal and provocative question arises as to whether or not there is a strong relationship between one's celebration of the sacrament of reconciliation and the level (degree) of truth at which one lives. The Gospels clearly associate Christ's acts of forgiveness with an increase of truth in the sinner's life.

Standing in the light is dangerous. Humankind seems to have always thought that darkness and the night would bring happiness; history and religion have proven otherwise. Only in the truth are we free; only in the light can we see; only in humility do we find true and lasting peace and love. Thomas Merton has pointed out the significance of honesty: "The beginning of love is truth, and before he will give us his love, God must cleanse our souls of the lies that are in them."

Over-seriousness vs. Humor

The ubiquitous mole-hill syndrome pervades many regions of human life. Involuntary peccadilloes become crushing burdens; small fears mushroom into life-and-death melodramas; suspicion subtitles the silences of our companions. Neglecting the context of words and events, being hypersensitive to ordinary exchanges, tending toward exaggeration—all of these are shortcuts to over-seriousness. Chandler's Uncle Remus gave wise counsel in suggesting in song that "everybody's got a laughing place." Yet even this place can be lost or forgotten. Children should not be allowed exclusive claim to the blessed prerogative of laughter.

The prosecuting attorney against humor bases his case on the historical circumstances of evil and suffering. His voice is bold and self-assured as he argues: "I bring before you the personal and collective sins of humankind. I present for your observation the injustices of war, the horror of abortion, the tragedies of mental illness and lingering disease. In the face of these dark, dreary, destructive realities, who could defend even a smile in human life, much less laughter and frivolity? Life is serious. Anyone proposing humor is simply manifesting unreasonableness if not insanity. The anguish and

pain which flood the world and the hearts of men and women prohibit forever not only the possibility of humor but also that of happiness."

The point is well taken. The realities of evil and suffering have
weighed heavily on human existence, but these events do not embrace all of life. There are the moments when lightness of heart,
quickness of mind, the incongruities of thought and word send the
human spirit into the ecstasy of laughter and joy.

Though the absence of humor might be attributed to the realities
of evil and suffering, another more subtle factor must be honestly
faced—over-work. The value of play, recreation and laughter can
easily be supplanted by one's professional functions and the basic
duties of daily life. Religious life, like any other walk of life, is vulnerable to this danger: the idol of activism. This is not to downgrade in
any way the value of work. Voltaire's insight should always be kept in
mind: "Work keeps at bay three great evils: boredom, vice and need."
Nevertheless, there has been a major value shift permitting competi-
tion and various forces of work to infiltrate even play and humor.
Play itself can become work; people come home from vacation to rest;
competitive recreation (cards, Monopoly, sports) must result in victory or else. The lightness, quickness, incongruities of life tend to disappear; fun has been infected by heaviness, slowness and rigidity.

William Blake's closing lines in his poem "Tiger, Tiger" hint at the
pleasant perspective that God has a sense of humor. After describing
the fierce attributes of the tiger, Blake beautifully contrasts these
qualities with the powerlessness and gentleness of a lamb. The subtle
implication reads:

> Did He smile his work to see,
> Did He who made the lamb, make thee?

Nathaniel Hawthorne, in "The Great Stone Face," allegorically
presents a similar image of a God who smiles on his creation. Humor
and humanness are allies, indeed; Christ, the image of the Father,
epitomizes all that humanness can be. To exclude humor does
violence to the humanity of Christ.

Psychologists have often associated humor with mental health.
One reason for this association lies in the fact that humor, in its apparent powerlessness, challenges some of the negative forces imping-
ing on human life. Anger can be eased with a gentle and courteous
wit; hostility wanes as the light of humor breaks down defensive
tendencies; unfounded fears, their rootlessness having been exposed,

dissipate before the smile of reassurance. True humor does not include in its family tree ridicule, sarcasm or mockery. Mental health decreases in proportion to their presence.

Several years ago I saw a cartoon depicting two men sitting at a bar. One of them, head thrown back, was laughing riotously. The caption, expressing the reflections of the second man, asked, "I wonder if he's laughing on the inside too?" A sense of humor must be an inside reality. It may well be that we have a basic moral obligation to foster humor in life. Some suggestions:

1) Share the humorous events of your life. In the course of a week many incongruities, extremely funny in nature, are often experienced. Sharing these experiences not only allows others to enjoy them vicariously, but also makes the narrator more sensitive to future humorous situations. Meals, spiced with stories about the foibles of life, are doubly enriching.

2) Read humorous works. James Thurber's *Secret Life of Walter Mitty*, C. S. Lewis's *Screwtape Letters*, Shakespeare's comedies as well as many of the works of Chesterton provide hours of relaxing and entertaining reading. The mind thus nourished becomes more aware of wit present in other dimensions of life.

3) Participate in recreative events. Personal involvement in games (pantomimes, plays, quasi-talent shows) can be highly recreative to the human spirit. The momentary joy of forgetting the burdens of life, the freeing experience of getting "lost" in play, the thrill of escaping time and space are hints of another type of time and way of life. The art of being foolish in play and humor helps foster spontaneity at other moments of life.

"Alone among the animals, he (man) is shaken with the beautiful madness called laughter; as if he caught sight of some secret in the very shape of the universe hidden from the universe itself." This is Chesterton's apt description of this amazing trait in human existence. With due apologies to hyenas, we humans alone have been blessed with this unique madness. Hopefully, such a blessing will not be lost nor give way to over-seriousness.

Simple solutions to the mystery of living are odious. The proposed "Ho-Ho, Hum-Hum" Principle (HOpe, HOspitality, HUMility, HUMor) cannot escape criticism. However, its redemption hinges on the fact that it is not as simplistic as it might appear, but is highly involved and complex. A principle attempts, but always fails, to capture the full essence of a perceived reality. The proposed principle challenges the discouragement, hostility, dishonesty and over-seriousness that threaten humanity. It is the living of the principle and the virtues of which it speaks that lead to true freedom.

12

Presence and Prepositions
Prepositional Christianity

Even as "generations have trod, have trod, have trod," English teachers have dutifully, if not eloquently, discoursed on the significance of language. I recall one such scholar who spoke eloquently of the nobility of the noun, the power and aggressiveness of the verb, the dynamic vitality of the adverb, the delightful color and warmth of the adjective. Continuing on through the other parts of speech, the teacher seemed to sing the praises of truly dear friends. However, the brilliant eulogy faltered when the *anawim*, the preposition, became the topic of conversation. This lowly creature was relegated to a functional role, given no existential identity of its own.

The preposition, I feel, can lead us into a deeper appreciation of some of the mysteries of our Christian faith. God, our Father, who graciously shares his life with us, does so in diverse ways. One of the most significant is that of his revealed work, Sacred Scripture. Here we come to see the revelation of his love and forgiveness.

One segment of Scripture is the preposition, which, if contemplated, can be a valuable means to probing more deeply the gift of grace. The purpose of the chapter is to show that three prepositions— *with*, *in*, and *for*—are subtle instruments depicting the mystery of Trinitarian love. These simple and common words convey a climate or atmosphere of *with*-ness, connoting the atmosphere of deep presence; *in*-ness, telling of our participation in the mystery of reality; *for*-ness, revealing a type of concern and generosity that creates growth and life.

Prepositional Christians are those who, in following Christ, achieve identity from the fact that God is *with* them, the Spirit dwells *in* them, and Christ, who is Lord, is totally *for* them. Experiencing this life of grace, these Christians in turn reach out to others by being *with* them in sharing life, by being involved *in* their lives through empathy, and by being *for* others in self-giving service. No longer is the preposition without dignity; precisely in its apparent obscurity it reveals a noble and strong power.

With-ness: God as Emmanuel

One of the most powerful and constant themes in all of Scripture is the consoling reality of God's presence in history, a presence which banishes fear. In Ps 118:5-7, we pray:

> In my straits I called upon the Lord,
>   the Lord answered me and set me free.
> The Lord is with me; I fear not;
>   what can man do against me?
> The Lord is with me to help me,
>   and I shall look down upon my foes.

The theme is repeated in the prophet Isaiah: "Do not be afraid, I am with you" (43:1). Again in the annunciation account Mary comes to know that "the Lord is with you . . . Mary, do not fear" (Luke 1:26-38). Zechariah's canticle states that since God has visited humankind we are now "free to worship him without fear" (Luke 1:74). The message is clear. God our Father is with humankind; in that presence fear vanishes and freedom is won. This is the history of salvation repeated time and time again in the lives of those who have eyes to see and ears to hear. With St. Paul all the people of God can cry out in the marvel of this mystery of God's nearness: "Rejoice in the Lord always! I say it again. Rejoice! (Phil 4:4)

The with-ness of God connotes an embracing atmosphere of profound and affective intimacy. Grounded in the rainbow promise made to Abraham and his descendants and reaffirmed in the Pentecost promise made by Jesus, this intimacy of God's nearness was firmly planted. Our present hope, confidence and strength lie in the same promise. Thus our faith is built on rock that provides an unshakable foundation, God's fidelity. Indeed, God is Emmanuel; for this, we praise and thank him.

Our Eucharistic liturgy continually reminds us of the with-ness of God. In the words of Scripture the events of God's interventions are

retold; in the reception of Christ in the sacrament we personally encounter the Lord; numerous times the celebrant proclaims, "The Lord
be with you"; just before Communion in a private prayer the priest
prays, "Let me never be parted from you." What is true of the
Eucharist is true of all liturgical life. In signs and symbols God keeps
drawing near to his people. Only our apartness and self-chosen alone-
ness prevents life from taking on its intended full meaning.

Having been made in God's image, we are challenged to live out the
quality of with-ness in our personal lives. The opportunities are many:
to be truly present to other people in their joys and sorrows; to listen
carefully to the hopes and fears of our fellow pilgrims in interior
silence; to gaze upon their suffering with compassion and gentleness.
Being an instrument of God's presence is at the very heart of the
Christian life. Anyone who has experienced the healing power of being in the presence of someone who really cares and is willing to give
time knows experientially what a tremendous gift with-ness is. I once
overheard the remark, "Whenever Mary is around, there is more life
and happiness. She is really present to people." Such a person incarnates the promised Spirit.

In an age cluttered with things and inundated with volumes of advice on how to do and be everything, simplicity draws us back to
prepositional living. The single reality of God's presence to us and the
call to share that gratuitous presence with others provides a source of
unity uncomplicated and integral, though not without its difficulties.
Struggles and problems will always abound in life; yet, this truth of
with-ness provides a philosophy of meaning whose validity is proven
in revelation and probably confirmed by our own intuition. Following
two such complementary sources, we have cause for confidence.

In-ness: Sharing in the Paschal Mystery

In a document published by the United States Catholic Conference
in 1973, spirituality was described as follows:

> Christian spirituality consists in the living out in experience,
> throughout the whole course of our lives, of the death-resurrection
> of Christ that we have been caught up into by baptism. It consists in
> living out in our day and in our lives the passage from sin and dark-
> ness to the light and warmth of God's gracious love. It is a process,
> whereby one rejects the tempting but illusory destructive forces
> that isolate and alienate man from his environment, his brothers, his
> God and himself in favor of accepting the free gift of God's life and
> love that allows him to stand erect, to rise above the pettiness of

egoism and the threat of the demonic and to live in freedom, in
strength, in gentleness and in love as a man of God. That is what the
spiritual life means for every Christian (*Spiritual Renewal of the
American Priesthood*, 3).

A key concept implicit in the above description and one which goes
as far back as Platonic philosophy is that of participation. Growth happens when people participate in truth, goodness and beauty. Participation means to be *in* something: in the center of a lecture, in the
heart of the home, in an exciting chapter of a book, in deep dialogue
with another. In the delightful and provocative book *Mister God, This
is Anna* (New York: Holt, Rinehart and Winston, 1974), the following
dialogue takes place between four-year-old Anna and the author,
Fynn:

> "Where do you know about me?"
> "Inside myself someplace."
> "Then you know my middle in your middle."
> "Yes, I suppose so."
> "Then you know Mister God in my middle in your middle, and every-
> thing you know, every person you know, you know in your middle.
> Every person and everything that you know has got Mister God in
> his middle, and so you have got his Mister God in your middle too.
> It's easy" (pp. 73–74).

The Christian, by definition, is invited to participate fully in the
life, death, resurrection and ascension of Christ. What happened in
the life of the historical Jesus and what is happening in the life of the
risen Lord now is to happen in some manner in my life. The pattern
will be the same; the circumstances will vary. Yet God still seeks to incarnate his love in the life of his children; God still draws people out of
the land of slavery to fear and sin and leads them into the freedom of
grace; God still heals, restores and comforts the poor and suffering of
the world. We are in the middle of all of this or we should be. Specta-
torship is light years from discipleship. The dialectics of being missioned will be ours: the cross but also the crown; the thorn as well as
the roses; darkness and light. Indeed, the prerogative of selective
Christianity is not ours nor has it been part of any authentic Christian
tradition. We share in the whole life of Christ: its emptying, dying and
rising.

Our freedom, that ambiguous titan, can be used to place us outside
the life of faith. The risen Lord does not force his governance on us;
we need not participate in the life of divine love and forgiveness. Our

sensate culture tries to rule us by locking us into the narrow confines of things; the academic world, noble and brilliant as it is, limits us, often unconsciously, to the boundaries of reason; the creative world of artistry tends to claim supremacy in its display of awesome beauty. To stop at any of these levels is to fall short of our true vocation. We are called to see and to act from within the relationship of faith, thereby giving to things, ideas and artifacts their true value and proper place. This in-ness of faith makes possible true wisdom, seeing things as they really are in all their beauty and truth. In-ness provides both perspective and power in that it brings about a transformation of our minds and our energies. Thus, as the clay of our life is molded into the image of Christ, we live a totally new existence in him. We are new creations.

Besides misguided freedom, our contemporary culture presents us with the destructive tendency towards superficiality. A cluttered life forces us to the surface of things and prohibits deep interiority. There are just so many things and ideas that a person can realistically cope with and properly integrate over a given period of time. In spite of this fact, our culture bombards us with innumerable stimuli that de- mand some type of response. More exactly, we expose ourselves to an unhealthy number of stimuli causing fragmentation of mind and heart. In-ness is threatened by gluttony at any level: physical obesity, psychological greed and spiritual avariciousness. Merry-go-round liv- ing precludes interior silence and shuns, above all things, the horrors of solitude. Little wonder that there is dissonance between ourselves and reality. Cluttered lives do not allow participation in the moment. In the face of reality being approached like the highly symbolic three- ring circus, some hard decisions and prudent priority judgments must be made if we are truly to live.

The challenge to our times and to our lives comes once again from the gospels. By sharing *in* Jesus' poverty we empty ourselves of those things that are unnecessary and that drain us of precious energy. Becoming poor in spirit and in truth creates in us the dispositions of openness and wonder. This poverty, symbolized by open hands, leads us to a healthy dependence on the Father's daily replenishment. The gifts we thus receive are to be passed on to others. It is precisely in giving away what we have that we gain the richness of God's life.

By sharing *in* the obedience of Jesus in his doing the Father's will, we foster the unity of all humans by becoming loving persons. Love reconciles and unites; unity blossoms into peace and joy. Obedience is that radical "yes" of Jesus to whatever the Father would ask, even death on a cross. Such is the obedience that we are invited to share in.

Then we are invited not only to share in the poverty and obedience of the Lord, but also *in* his risen life which is a now mystery. By doing this we witness to the fulness of the paschal mystery. The apparitions of the risen Lord point to the characteristics of this mode of existence: gracious charm, restored hope, profound peace and exuberant joy. The disciples on the road to Emmaus and Mary of Magdala experienced the fulness of the paschal mystery because they shared in the poverty and obedience of Jesus. Our constant prayer should be the hymn recorded by St. Paul in his letter to the Philippians (2:6-11). It is a summa of in-ness!

For-ness: Eucharistizing

In the spring of the year, the sap deeply embedded in the roots of the maple tree begins its gradual and growth-filled journey through the tree. The warmth of the sun dispels winter's dormancy. Those who enter the presence of someone who is really *for* them come to life and develop at an incredible rate. For-ness is the spring sun causing creativity and personal enrichment. The gift of faith allows us to experience the precious reality that God is not only with and in us, but that he is totally *for* us. In our human relationships we can be with someone whose trustworthiness is not assured; we can be invited to participate in an undertakng that can ultimately destroy. For-ness is not absolutely necessary. However, our relationship with God includes not only presence and participation in healthy adventures but also the assurance that he is unconditionally *for* us. This follows from God's nature: he is love, as St. John tells us. The active side of love is being concerned for others, concerned about their growth.

The Eucharist provides ample evidence demonstrating God's love. "This is my body given for you. This is my blood to be shed for you." This excentration exemplifies the diffusiveness of divine grace. The focus of Jesus' consciousness was on the mission entrusted to him by the Father: to bring all creation back to the Father. We can pray with St. Paul that confident reflection, "If God is for us, who is against us?" (Rom 8:31)

At this point a major difficulty might arise. There is an erroneous but nonetheless powerful tendency in the mind of some to think that God does not really like us. Not only is he not for us, he is *against us!* (Or, because of jealousy, we are competitively against him.) Though

Scripture and the Church doctrine teach otherwise, the inner dis-ordering of our lives can construct an image of God at once false and devastating. Whether these false images come from childhood experi-ence, distorted teaching or personal fantasizing, the underlying and perhaps not uncommon doubt about God's for-ness might well be one of the many expressions of original sin. By contrast, the image of God presented in Fynn's work quoted earlier tells of someone who had ex-perienced God's for-ness:

> Anna was not only deeply in love with Mister God; she was proud of him. Anna's pride in Mister God grew and grew to such dimensions that in some idiot moment I wondered if Mister God ever went pink with pleasure. Whatever feelings people have had about Mister God over the many centuries, I'm very sure of one thing—nobody has ever liked Mister God more than Anna (p. 36).

The light and truth of God's concern for us mandates us to be for others in service. By definition we are Eucharistic people and that means giving our lives regardless of the cost. This for-ness is no abstract reality. It is a matter of flesh and bone besides good inten-tions. We must incarnate our for-ness by protecting the rights of the defenseless, by giving time and energy to the needy, by reaching out to the lonely and distressed, by sharing our insights in conversation, by performing the small courtesies of life, by smiling through tears and fears, by laughing with others in relativizing undue worries. For-ness is as concrete as a call for Zaccheus to come down from a tree and as painful as Peter's tears of repentance. The Father and Son have sent their Spirit into our hearts that we might be for others just as the Trinity has been for us.

In a classroom, or in any situation for that matter, there are three realities: the experience of sensible things (faces, voices, odor); the level of consciousness (awareness, meaning, insight); and then the at-mosphere or climate that pervades those educational walls. None of the three can be denied as being real; however, the atmosphere and climate are perhaps the most powerful. Prepositions tell of a climate: the climate of presence through with-ness; the climate of participa-tion through in-ness; the climate of generosity through for-ness. The term "spirit" can also be used to convey the same realities: the spirit of the here and now, the spirit of involvement, the spirit of love. God's Spirit is prepositional in that it causes and sustains relationships. We come through the gift of the Spirit to experience the wide circles of in-terdependence and interrelatedness of all of life. Prepositions are the relational words to describe this life.

The search for identity underscores the importance of prepositional thinking. Our identity is gained only in the context of our relationships. Because God is with, in and for us we come to see that we are his children who share fully his life. The doxology at the end of the Eucharistic Prayer says it all: "Through him, with him, in him, in the unity of the Holy Spirit, all glory and honor is yours, almighty Father, for ever and ever!"

13

Presence and Play
Ministry of Surprise

In the presence of a carefully wrapped package, a certain light glows in the eyes of a child, be that child four or forty. A gift to be opened: the excitement, the wonder, the anticipation, the surprise of it all! Then, as trembling fingers toss bow, string and paper aside, the glow bursts into a flame of "wow!"—and immediately the gift and all its hidden love wrap the child in tender embrace and emotion.

To the observant spectator present at birthday parties, anniversary celebrations, Christmas eve festivities, a question must be asked: who is more excited—the recipient or the giver? The glow in the child's eye may well be dim in comparison with the burning love in the one who has created this moment of joy.

To be a giver is certainly part of everyone's Christian ministry, for the Lord himself so often surprised his disciples and his people with marvelous gifts of health and joy, freedom and faith. These gifts often came in hidden, unexpected ways: being called to a full life by leaving all behind, obtaining peace through suffering, coming to faith in the darkness of the crucifixion. Jesus served by surprise, a special style of ministry much needed today in a world so highly managed and computerized that the mystery of surprise has become an endangered species.

This chapter has as its immediate goal to outline a theology of surprise and to state some requirements demanded of a minister of surprise. Its remote goal is to create a national refuge for all ministers of surprise who, having given their unexpected gifts, can scurry back to this haven for protection from grateful recipients and for time to package the next surprise that the Lord wants to give through them.

Theology of Surprise

Any understanding of ministry must be based on our concept of God. The Scriptures reveal numerous facets of God's generosity, and three of these in particular may well serve as a foundation for a ministry of surprise. These are the mysteries of creation, incarnation, and resurrection.

Is not creation a surprise and our Father a surpriser? A universe so vast we cannot count the stars! Planets that dance around a rather insignificant star! Animals created strictly for laughter: welcome the giraffe and hyena! And the caterpillar who incredibly would like to fly, and does! Water that gets angry and steams off, then becomes silent and locks itself in ice! Small yellow manufacturers of honey with sour stings! And then, that creature with body and soul, time and eternity, freedom and determinism, knowledge and ignorance, grace and sin—all mixed into one! Wow!

Is not the incarnation a surprise and Jesus the surpriser? Love enfleshed in one like us! God-become-man! The human condition deliberately and lovingly assumed in all its fulness! A hidden, humble, silent life! A few years of ministry, then a scandalous death! A life of many failures, rejections and anguished betrayals! A Lord who suffers and goes to the cross out of love. Wow!

Is not the resurrection a surprise and the Spirit of the Father and Son a surpriser? A Spirit of life flowing from death! A new presence after the "finality" of death! A power released from the powerlessness of the cross! Hope flowing through hearts of those despairing on pilgrim roads and in empty gardens! Courage given to the cowardly! Peace healing fragmented souls and fearful friends! The bond of sin and death broken forever! Wow!

In an unexpected way, God as *the* minister of surprise breaks into history with a suddenness that staggers our finite imagination and intellect, with the possibility (to be realized in time) of rejection of the gift of himself, with the desire that all gifted people would treasure the love offered and come to a life of deep mutuality in him.

Though history gives volumes of evidence that many have not acknowledged the surprises of creation, incarnation, and resurrection, there have always been some who have been open to these gifts and have rejoiced in the mystery of God's love. Julian of Norwich was such a one:

And in this [God] showed me something small, no bigger than a hazelnut, lying in the palm of my hand, as it seemed to me, and it was as round as a ball. I looked at it with the eye of my understanding and thought: What can this be? I was amazed that it could last, for I thought that because of its littleness it would suddenly have fallen into nothing. And I was answered in my understanding: It lasts and always will, because God loves it; and thus everything has being through the love of God.

In this little thing I saw three properties. The first is that God made it, the second is that God loves it, the third is that God preserves it. But what did I see in it? It is that God is the Creator and the protector and the lover. For until I am substantially united to him, I can never have perfect rest or true happiness, until, that is, I am so attached to him that there can be no created thing between my God and me.[1]

The God of surprises continues throughout history to amaze us in sudden and unexpected ways. Hopefully we have the sense and sensitivity to respond.

Made in his image and likeness, we are challenged to minister to each other and the world as God has ministered to us: creatively, incarnationally and "resurrectionally." The specific form of how this will happen is not essential; the fact that we are willing to serve is. Often the effectiveness of service will be in proportion to its simplicity and littleness. A model of this might be the experience of Annie Dillard as a young girl:

When I was six or seven years old, growing up in Pittsburgh, I used to take a precious penny of my own and hide it for someone else to find. It was a curious compulsion; sadly, I've never been seized by it since. For some reason I always "hid" the penny along the same stretch of sidewalk up the street. I would cradle it at the roots of a sycamore, say, or in a hole left by a chipped-off piece of sidewalk. Then I would take a piece of chalk, and, starting at either end of the block, draw huge arrows leading up to the penny from both directions. After I learned to write I labeled the arrows: *Surprise Ahead* or *Money This Way*. I was greatly excited, during all this arrow-drawing, at the thought of the first lucky passerby who would receive in this way, regardless of merit, a free gift from the universe. But I never lurked about. I would go straight home and not give the matter another thought, until, some months later, I would be gripped again by the impulse to hide another penny.[2]

Silas Marner found and hoarded many pennies; the Christian finds and shares the gifts received. One form of sharing is to repackage the gift with excitement and glee, hide it in strange and delightful places, and not wait around to be acknowledged as the giver.

This is the ministry of surprise, a ministry done out of love and without immediate compensation. And yet the compensation is quite immediate—the more gifts we give away, the more clearly we are able to spot the chalk marks pointing to cracks or around corners: *Surprise Ahead.* New gifts to be discovered and shared.

The Unexpected. The tripod upon which the ministry of surprise rests is the unexpected, the unpredictable, and the unnecessary. First of all, the unexpected. Surprise is the term we give to those experiences in which a person is forcibly impressed because the gift or event is unexpected; it catches one off guard. While expecting a routine response, something else is forthcoming. Many proverbs contain this element of surprise:

> If I die, I forgive you; if I recover, we shall see.
> He who would speak the truth must have one foot in the stirrup.
> If three people say you are an ass, put on the bridle.[3]

As we turn to our faith, we see Jesus consistently speaking the unexpected: if you want to be happy, be poor in spirit; if you want to have the fulness of life, die to yourself; if you send out invitations for lunch and dinner, invite the lame and the blind, those who cannot repay you; if you want to be great, serve; love your enemies; turn the other cheek; pray for those who persecute you.

In this series of succinct adages Jesus packages the wisdom of his Father. He spoke what he heard; he spoke what was in his heart; he spoke what he lived. Jesus himself was the surprise, the unexpected one who forcibly impressed those whom he met because they were taken off guard. Sad to say, many could not accept this Surpriser and walked back to the expected, complacent, routine life of boredom, anxiety, and ennui.

Creativity, creation's source, contains the essential component of the unexpected. J. Bronowski describes the creative process in these terms:

> A man becomes creative, whether he is an artist or a scientist, when he finds a new unity in the variety of nature. He does so by finding a likeness between things which were not thought alike before, and this gives him a sense at the same time of richness and of understanding. The creative mind is a mind that looks for unexpected likenesses.[4]

In another essay he states: "To my mind, it is a mistake to think of creative activity as something unusual. I hold that the creative activity is normal to all living things."[5] Thus God has implanted in all of us the creative seed that he himself enfleshed in his own creative act. Creation must be classified as an unexpected mystery. So, too, the incarnation and resurrection: events that catch us off guard and cause the mind to falter and the heart to rejoice.

The Unpredictable. Unpredictability, the second element of surprise, reveals something of the interior life of the minister of surprise. Therein resides a magical process which changes the natural flow of things, even to the extent of influencing the final working out of the formula. The story begun finds its ending during the telling; the expression of concern adjusts itself as new and varied needs arise; the plan contains an open-endedness allowing the influence of diverse circumstances.

Various historical figures exemplify this unpredictable element of surprise. O. Henry, in the short story; St. Francis, in religion; Newton, in science. In praising the positive side of unpredictability, the importance and necessity of predictability is not denied; an orderly and peaceful life has need of this ingredient. However, even here there is plenty of room for the unpredictable. Life demands a balance of each. "Life is a series of surprises, and would not be worth taking or keeping if it were not. God delights to isolate us every day, and hide from us the past and the future."[6]

Unpredictability lies behind the mysteries of creation, incarnation, and resurrection. Even Jimmy the Greek would have erred, if only by a few points, with the conjecture that God would have seen fit to create a universe and a people out of love; that God would assume unto himself the human condition and all its joys and pains; that death and sin would be conquered because of loving obedience and the result of that surrender. These ongoing mysteries are so incomprehensible that even the greatest fiction writers falter in trying to imagine such events. In the face of all this unpredictability of God, St. Paul can only praise, not explain what has happened:

> How rich are the depths of God—how deep his wisdom and knowledge—and how impossible to penetrate his motives or understand his methods! Who could ever know the mind of the Lord? Who could ever be his counsellor? Who could ever give him anything or lend him anything? All that exists comes from him; all is by him and for him. To him be glory for ever! Amen (Rom 11:33-36).

Those who serve the unpredictable God have an interesting challenge. Perhaps the unpredictable, creative dialogue with fellow pilgrims will foster truth where before there was only doubt and confusion. Perhaps the mandate will become clear to enflesh love in unpredictable, incarnational ways through verbalizing deep concern ("I love you more than word can wield the matter"[7]), or by being a clown in a world of heaviness and suffering, or by bringing warmth to frigid, frightened hearts. The one who serves an unpredictable God also journeys with the risen Lord, a Lord who consoles and brings hope to the sorrowing and discouraged. In disguise we make his joyful presence felt wherever people are in want and pain.

The Unnecessary. The surprise tripod has a third leg: the unnecessary. One can eat a meal without condiments; one can live in a house without flowers; one can journey throughout life without celebrations. One can, but only at the high cost of lost joy and delight. Surprises are gratuitous, as is all grace. They need not be, they are contingent. Yet life would be dreary without them, and we all know that survival is far different from living. Life without surprises is merely minimal existence. Recently a friend of mine commented: "I don't have any ha-ha's!" Interpreted: my life is devoid of surprises, and I'm hurting.

God did not have to create, to become one of us, to bless us with the gift of resurrection. That he did in no way takes away from the gratuity of these mysteries. No necessity can be ascribed to such events of faith. What this highlights is that at the core of the unnecessity of surprise is love. Love cannot be forced or demanded; it bursts forth where "it will flame out, like shining from shook foil; it gathers to a greatness, like the ooze of oil crushed."[8]

Though it might be argued that love necessarily must give of itself, there is no forcing the manner of expression. The manner is unexpected, unpredictable and unnecessary: God is love but he need not have loved in the three life mysteries that we are dealing with here. What other forms that love might have assumed can only be guessed at by the highly imaginative.

Those who serve the gratuitous God are given a marvelous freedom to minister in ways that are not specifically "necessary." How one expresses the mysteries of creation, incarnation, and resurrection in one's ministry is surprisingly flexible. This freedom of unnecessary specificity reveals the beauty of the mutuality between creator and creature: God calls us to responsibility but allows us freedom (the heart of surprise) in distributing the gifts that we have received in diverse patterns.

As instruments of grace and channels of peace we must carefully discern the form and manner of how our Father has dealt with us and then we go forth, with the same unexpectedness, unpredictability, and unnecessity to continue the same work. The Spirit has been given to us to undertake this work: the Spirit of surprise. All this is sheer grace for us and for those with whom we work.

Two examples of persons who ministered in surprising ways should help to concretize our subject. Both individuals were recipients of surprises; both then became ministers of surprises by sharing the gifts received in unexpected ways. To know such people and to travel with them are both a source of courage and a constant reminder of the possibilities of exciting and diverse ministries. These ministers of surprise are C. S. Lewis and Teresa of Avila.

Lewis knew the experience of surprise so well from his own life that he entitled his autobiography *Surprised by Joy*. His journey is the movement of a soul from an amorphous atheism to a dynamic faith. God broke into his life unexpectedly, unpredictably, and unnecessarily. Apparently it was no easy task for God:

> The Prodigal Son at least walked home on his own feet. But who can duly adore that Love which will open the high gates to a prodigal who is brought in kicking, struggling, resentful, and darting his eyes in every direction for a chance of escape.[9]

Even before this reluctant return, God was preparing the heart of Lewis for his love. That preparation came through a stirring desire that God instilled in Lewis' heart by means of nature.

> It troubled me with what I can only describe as the Idea of Autumn. It sounds fantastic to say that one can be enamored of a season, but that is something like what happened; and, as before, the experience was one of intense desire. And one went back to the book, not to gratify the desire . . . but to reawaken it.[10]

God surprises us through nature, through human interactions, through prayer, through sacraments—through life. Lewis was drawn by the stirrings of God in his deepest, truest self.

God called C. S. Lewis to the ministry of writing, and it was here that the author would share many surprises with others in surprising ways. Lewis planted many pennies that led to God. Unsuspectingly people would pick up Lewis' space trilogy (*Out of the Silent Planet, Perelandra, That Hideous Strength*) only to discover too late that throughout this "science fiction" the God of surprises was constantly present and at work. A single selection from each work provides an example:

> "He (the Old One) is not that sort," said Hnohra, "that he has to live anywhere," . . .[11]
>
> To walk out of His will is to walk nowhere.[12]
>
> What awaited her there was serious to the degree of sorrow and beyond. There was no form nor sound. The mould under the bushes, the moss on the path, and the little brick border, were not visibly changed. But they were changed. A boundary had been crossed. She had come into a world, or into a Person, or into the presence of a Person. Something expectant, patient, inexorable, met her with no veil or protection between. In the closeness of that contact she perceived at once that the Director's words had been entirely misleading. This demand which now pressed upon her was not, even by analogy, like any other demand. It was the origin of all right demands and contained them. In its light you could understand them . . . It was a person . . . yet also a thing, a made thing, made to please Another and in Him to please all others . . .[13]

A work that was more directly theological, *The Screwtape Letters*, offered through the guise of humor much insight into the workings of the human spirit in the spiritual domain. Again Lewis catches the reader off guard as the author challenges people to examine their own struggle with temptation and the quality of their relationship with God and each other:

> To be greatly and effectively wicked a man needs some virtue.[14]
>
> We must picture Hell as a state where everyone is perpetually concerned about his own dignity and advancement, where everyone has a grievance, and where everyone lives the deadly serious passions of envy, self-importance, and resentment.[15]
>
> When He (God) talks of their losing their selves, He means only abandoning the clamour of self-will.[16]

Perhaps best of all, in the *Chronicles of Narnia*, a seven-volume series of supposedly children's literature, the magic of surprise and creativity is most sensitively developed. In these works Lewis tells of the adventures of four children into a strange and mysterious land, Narnia. Behind the screen of fiction an entire interpretation of salvation history is presented. In unexpected and unpredictable ways, God intervenes in the lives of these little people and manifests his love and concern. The lion Aslan, symbolic of Christ, is constantly breaking into their lives, offering them support and life:

And Lucy felt running through her that deep shiver of gladness which you only get if you are being solemn and still.[17]

"Who *are* you?" asked Shasta.

"Myself," said the Voice (Lion's), very deep and low so that the earth shook; and again "Myself," loud and clear and gay: and then the third time "Myself," whispered so softly you could hardly hear it, and yet it seemed to come from all around you as if the leaves rustled with it.[18]

The memory of that moment stayed with them, so that as long as they both lived, if ever they were sad or afraid or angry, the thought of all that golden goodness (Lion), and the feeling that it was still there, quite close, just round some corner or just behind some door, would come back and make them sure, deep down inside, that all was well.[19]

Through the gift of literature, C. S. Lewis imaged the three life mysteries of our faith. His stories contain a rich creative element, bringing life to many by means of insight and understanding; his writings incarnated in concrete images and refined ideas God's gracious love and concern; his theology and fiction have helped the confused rise from their despondency to a fuller and richer life. Surprised by joy indeed; the gift received graciously given.

The buoyancy and spontaneity of Teresa of Avila tell of a personality who delighted in life and enjoyed surprises. Despite the weight of helping her community to reform, Teresa's life and work contained elements of the unexpected, unpredictable, and unnecessary. She was surprised by the ways of God; her ways surprised many and continue to do so in the influence of her writings:

. . . my God is not in the least meticulous . . .[20]

. . . we need no wings to go in search of Him but only to find a place where we can be alone and look upon Him present within us. Nor need we feel strange in the presence of so kind a Guest; we must talk to Him humbly, as we should to our Father, ask Him for things as we should ask a father, tell Him our troubles, beg Him to put them right, and yet realize that we are not worthy to be called His children.[21]

Briefly, in this tempest, there is no help for it but to wait upon the mercy of God, Who suddenly, at the most unlooked for hour, with a single word, or on some chance occasion, lifts the whole of this burden from the soul, so that it seems as if it has never been clouded over, but is full of sunshine and far happier than it was before.[22]

These authors like many others depict a certain style of life that breaks down the ordinary and routine, exposing us to broader vistas.

Authentic life cannot be contained by traditional expression or behavioral patterns but seeks new and dynamic ways of sharing its vitality and energy. God's grandeur does "flame out"; incredible that our blindness is so complete, our deafness so severe.

Only the dynamite of surprise can loosen the hard-packed soil cutting off air and moisture; only the unexpected and unpredictable can catch us off guard and awaken us to the fulness of life; only the unnecessary can help us see what is really necessary and essential. Our God is a God of surprises; we who are made to his image and likeness are its ministers.

Qualifications for the Ministry of Surprise

Undoubtedly, the official Church will never sanction an office or a ministry of surprise; there will be no ordination rite for clowns. But if there were one, I would like to suggest the following qualifications for all candidates:

1. *The minister must be able to plant pennies.*

   Thus, possession of pennies is a prerequisite. These would include such items as stories, jokes, insights, small gifts, smiles, tears, dreams, ideals, soft eyes, etc.

2. *The minister must be able to plant and run.*

   Candidates are disqualified if they stay around to watch the gift being discovered. One must be able to live without immediate compensation. Underlying this qualification is the fact that too much precious time is lost by staying around; other gifts may never be planted because of such delaying tactics.

3. *The minister must be surprise-able.*

   The inability to receive is an impediment to this office within the Church. The minister is one who is sent; not being able to receive implies a lack of authentic contact with the Sender.

4. *The minister must be purged of avarice.*

   The greatest danger for the minister of surprise is to retain the pennies given by the Lord. A second serious danger is to desire more than what is beneficial to oneself and others. The retention of surprise pennies causes oppressiveness; the constant desire for more and more pennies fosters a discontent that makes everyone nervous, even God.

5. *The minister must be involved in an ongoing education program.*

   The assumption behind this requirement is that hearts tend to harden, muscles tend to atrophy, languages are lost, unless each of these is properly exercised and nurtured. These educational units would be acceptable:

a. daily reading of cartoons (1 credit)
b. standing on one's head for five minutes every week—helps give new perspectives (½ credit)
c. traveling on back roads (1¼ credits)
d. reading Don Quixote (2 credits)
e. watching sunsets (1 credit)
f. hugging the huggable (1½ credits)

Our Theme Confirmed. In such a serious theological work as Jon Sobrino's *Christology at the Crossroads,* we find the theme of surprise verified: "It is the Father who is at work in history, and he works through human beings. He discloses his will in unexpected ways, carrying it out in ways that are a source of scandal to the world. With this realization Jesus turns to the Father and offers him thanks."[23]

We see in our God the very element that takes us off guard: the unexpected. We cannot control and manage him; his ways and thoughts are not ours. How delightful and exciting this is—to be ministers of such a reality in our own times, regardless of the scandal it might cause. The staid are many, the surprisers, few.

Ever so often those musical words are heard: "What a pleasant surprise to see you" or "Let's throw a surprise party for Sarah!" Ever so often the sidewalks are chalked with the bold letters *Surprise Ahead.* Ever so often people are overwhelmed with laughter. Know that in these events ministers of surprise are around and active. In and through them comes life; God's mysteries of creation, incarnation, and resurrection are made visible. And one day all these ministers and their graced followers will experience what Julian of Norwich so accurately describes in her vision of heaven:

> And in this my understanding was lifted up into heaven, where I saw the Lord God as a lord in his own house, who has called all his friends to a splendid feast. Then I did not see him seated anywhere in his own house; but I saw him reign in his house as a king, and fill it all full of joy and mirth, gladdening and consoling his dear friends with himself, very familiarly and courteously, with wonderful melody in endless love in his own fair blissful countenance, which glorious countenance fills all heaven full of the joy and bliss of the divinity.[24]

1. Julian of Norwich, *Showings*, translated with an introduction by Edmund Colledge, O.S.A., and James Walsh, S.J. (New York: Paulist Press, 1978) 183.

2. Annie Dillard, *Pilgrim at Tinker Creek* (New York: Bantam Books, Inc., 1974) 15–16.

3. See John W. Gardner and Francesa Gardner Reese, *Know or Listen to Those Who Know* (New York: W. W. Norton & Company, Inc., 1975) 231, 233, 149.

4. J. Bronowski, "The Creative Process," *A Sense of the Future* (Cambridge, Mass.: The MIT Press, 1977) 16.

5. *Ibid.*, "On Art and Science" 16.

6. Ralph W. Emerson, *Experience* (New York: Heritage Press, 1941) 149.

7. William Shakespeare, *King Lear*, Act I, Sc. i.

8. Gerard Manley Hopkins, "God's Grandeur."

9. C. S. Lewis, *Surprised by Joy* (New York: Harcourt, Brace & World, Inc., 1955) 229.

10. *Ibid.* 16–17.

11. C. S. Lewis, *Out of the Silent Planet* (New York: Macmillan Publishing Co., Inc., 1965) 68.

12. C. S. Lewis, *Perelandra* (New York: Macmillan Publishing Co., Inc., 1944) 116.

13. C. S. Lewis, *That Hideous Strength* (New York: Macmillan Publishing Co., Inc., 1946) 318.

14. C. S. Lewis, *The Screwtape Letters* (New York: Macmillan Publishing Co., Inc., 1961) 135.

15. *Ibid.* ix.

16. *Ibid.* 59.

17. C. S. Lewis, *The Lion, the Witch and the Wardrobe* (New York: Macmillan Publishing Co., Inc., 1954) 103.

18. C. S. Lewis, *The Horse and His Boy* (New York: Macmillan Publishing Co., Inc., 1954) 158.

19. C. S. Lewis, *The Magician's Nephew* (New York: Macmillan Publishing Co., Inc., 1954) 179.

20. *The Complete Works of St. Theresa of Jesus*, trans. E. Allison Peers, II (London: Sheed and Ward, 1946) 98.

21. *Ibid.* 114.

22. *Ibid.* 273.

23. Jon Sobrino, S.J., *Christology at the Crossroads*, trans. John Drury (Maryknoll, N.Y.: Orbis Books, 1978) 155.

24. Julian of Norwich, *Showings* 203.

14

Presence and Pragmatism
Qualities and Responsibilities
of a Chapter Delegate

The significance of general chapters of religious communities cannot be overstressed. The responsibility of providing and sustaining a vision, the challenge to be true to the gospel while preserving the uniqueness of the community's special charism, the mandate to read the signs of the times and yet have a universal sensitivity: all demand diligent work and competent deliberators. This chapter is an attempt to describe some of the qualities inherently crucial to the fulfillment of the above challenges and to specify areas of responsibility following upon election as a delegate to a general chapter. Essentially what is being offered is a job description, a delineation of the functions of a trusted steward. The thesis of this chapter is that a chapter delegate is called to be a dialogical person, a prophetic person, and a wounded healer.[1]

Delegate: A Dialogical Person

God our Father is a God of revelation. In the precious mystery of his grace, he has chosen to reveal himself and his gracious love to mankind. Throughout history God has communicated with his people, calling all creation to life and fidelity. As a dialogical God, he longs to speak his love and forgiveness; he searches out those who will listen and respond to his word. God has spoken and told us where he is and who he is. We are called to imitate our Father: "Try, then, to imitate God, as children of his that he loves . . ." (Eph 5:1); we do this from one perspective by becoming dialogical persons. Our model is the Father who shares himself with us in word and sacrament.

The qualities of a dialogical person are many; we will limit our consideration to three essential attitudes that must be present if authentic communication is to happen. The first and perhaps most difficult quality of a dialogical person is *listening*. Monologues are terribly common in life: empty, one-sided discourses in which no one is listening and probably no one is thinking. Dialogue demands attentive listening, feeling behind the words into the reality being expressed. This type of listening is concerned not with simple, audible comprehension but with a compassionate desire to enter into the world of the speaker to see what has been seen, to hear what has been given. An example of this sensitive listening can be found in Tolstoy's classic *War and Peace:*

> He told of these adventures as he had never yet recalled them. He now, as it were, saw a new meaning in all he had gone through. Now that he was telling it all to Natasha he experienced that pleasure which a man has when women listen to him—not clever women who when listening either try to remember what they hear to enrich their minds and when opportunity offers to retell it, or who wish to adopt it to some thought of their own and promptly contribute their own clever comments prepared in their own little mental workshop —but the pleasure given by real women gifted with a capacity to select and absorb the very best a man shows of himself. Natasha without knowing it was all attention: she did not lose a word, nor a single quiver in Pierre's voice, no look, no twitch of a muscle in his face, nor a single gesture. She caught the unfinished word in its flight and took it straight into her open heart, divining the secret meaning of all Pierre's mental travail.[2]

If a delegate is truly to listen, there must be some degree of interior silence. Turning off the inner engines is difficult and demands discipline, yet so necessary if the message is to be understood and the feelings are to be appreciated. C. S. Lewis expressed well our dilemma: "Inner silence is for our race a difficult achievement."[3] To obtain this silence we must deal with our own fears, insecurities and prejudices. These tendencies block listening, put us into the land of defensiveness and create a sense of being threatened. Secure in our forts, with drawbridge raised and the moat filled with crocodiles, we protect ourselves from new ideas, visions and possibilities. Again C. S. Lewis drives home the point: "He could never empty, or silence, his own mind to make room for an alien thought."[4] A chapter delegate must listen and discern. Electing a nondialogical person to a chapter is like inviting a deaf person to a concert or taking someone who is blind to an art museum. Neither experience nor growth is possible if essential capacities are lacking. Listening is essential to dialogue.

A second quality of a dialogical person is *trust*. In an essay written in 1952, Martin Buber stated: "But here is an essential presupposition for all this dialogue: it is necessary to overcome the massive distrust in others and also that in ourselves."[5] If Buber's observation is correct—and there seems to be sufficient evidence to verify his reflection—we have a lot of growing to do. We must reestablish trust in others and in ourselves. Hopefully, we will ground our trust on the theological fact that God has faith and trust in us. He has given us freedom and intelligence, blessed us with insight and grace. We are his stewards entrusted to do his work in our times. Sensing this, a delegate must come to a radical trust in his own personal insight and conviction. This trust must then be extended to others who are also on the journey searching for truth and goodness. Nothing breaks down communication so quickly as distrust; it hardly pays to initiate a discussion unless there is a solid degree of self-confidence and a climate of confidence in others. Buber, quoting Robert Hutchins, writes: "The essence of the Civilization of the Dialogue is communication. This presupposes mutual respect and understanding, it does not presuppose agreement."[6] Our trust in self and others must be supplemented with respect and the ability to understand. It would be profitable for delegates to spend some time critically reading Emerson's essay "Self-Reliance" and Howe's *Miracle of Dialogue*.

Desire for truth is a third quality of the dialogical person. A longing for insight and perspective characterizes the mind and heart of a truth-seeker. Like an ink blotter, this type of person quickly and completely absorbs truth wherever it presents itself. Desire for truth means being in contact with facts (hard data). There is no excuse for ignorance; the homework must be done. Besides researching and interpreting facts, truth demands contact with basic principles, those patterns of meanings which explain and elucidate reality. Experience and reflection are prerequisites here. Besides dealing with facts and principles, desire for truth calls for the basic disposition manifesting a willingness to change and grow. Regardless of who speaks—a "pagan" philosopher, a formed provincial, a member in one's local community, a poet—the searcher for truth listens and evaluates. So often God is speaking through these and other historical channels. If the search is honest, change will be demanded; certain pet categories will be dropped and new ones added (e.g., collegiality); treasured prejudices must be let go and openness of mind fostered; static rigid formulations must be reexamined in the light of new research and insight. The process is painful and not without its victims but this is the price of honest discipleship.

If a chapter delegate is called to imitate God by being a dialogical person characterized by attentive listening, deep trust and a desire for truth, several responsibilities automatically arise. (1) A chapter delegate must be *available* to the people he or she represents. The thinking, feeling and life-style of the constituency must be familiar material to the delegate. The duty of being available is not without its price: time and energy, precious and limited commodities, must be sacrificed in fulfilling this obligation. (2) A chapter delegate must be *able to make distinctions.* Meriol Trevor, in her biography of Cardinal Newman, wrote concerning Fr. Faber: "He would never distinguish between disapproval and dislike; he himself always spoke of hating people who disagreed with him and he could not believe others were different."[7] This type of person should not be allowed to be in the arena of policy making. One must be able to know and experience the difference between understanding and agreeing, between a person and an issue, between an idea and its emotive force. Chapters in which such distinctions are consistently made result in community growth and peace. (3) A chapter delegate must be *willing to speak* during the chapter proceedings. Some eloquent (and not so eloquent) discourses on stairways and in other private areas would be more profitably shared with the entire group. There is no excuse for devastating criticisms made outside the halls of the chapter room and silence reigning within. As a general principle one should not say outside of chapter what one is not willing to say to the whole group. A delegate is mandated to speak out, to take a stance, to express points of view. If this is done with respect and in the spirit of truth, there should be little to fear. Merton's insight is helpful: "Ignorance is the parent of fear."[8] Our talk should flow from our study and reflection on life.

Delegate: A Prophetic Person

Jesus was a prophet. The study of Scripture verifies this fact and further points out that throughout the Old Testament the Father sent prophets on special missions. Jesus' mission was unique and yet contained the basic ingredients of those who preceded him: to reveal who the Father was and also to provide the means whereby people might return to the Father. Like Christ, the chapter delegate is missioned. This "being sent" comes through the community and the task flowing from this mission resembles that of all the prophets. The booklet *Spiritual Renewal of the American Priesthood* describes the prophet in these terms: "The prophet's function was to perceive the presence or absence of God in situations and to point out the consequences of that presence or absence. A prophet had to know contemporary issues, but even more, he had to be sensitive to the mind and will of God."[9]

In the context of this prophetic role, certain traits clearly emerge that would characterize a chapter delegate. The first of these is *sensitivity*. This sensitivity must embrace the three sectors of time: the past with its treasures and cultural limitations, the present with its high ideals and ambiguous facts, the future with its plans and realistic hopes. It is possible and often happens in life that we eat but do not taste, read but do not comprehend, listen but do not hear. Historical insensitivity cannot be excused; we must be in touch with our roots and our traditions. Unless carefully nurtured, this sensitivity can be lost. Sensitivity demands that we perceive what is happening here and now; that we enter into or are caught up by the present moment. This is not just a cognitive apprehension since it necessarily includes an affective involvement. The future will be basically meaningless if we do not avoid the tragedy of lost sensitivity written of by Hopkins:

> Generations have trod, have trod, have trod;
>   And all is seared with trade; bleared, smeared with toil;
>   And wear man's smudge and shares man's smell; the soul
> Is bare now, nor can foot feel, being shod.[10]

It is time once again to take off our shoes,[11] to be sensitive to our world, to our people, to our deepest self. A sense of reverence, awe and wonder is much needed in our merry-go-round world.

Prophets are, of necessity, *courageous* people. If Emerson is correct in saying that "God will not make himself manifest to cowards,"[12] then the virtue of fortitude takes on added importance in fostering the kingdom. Among the courageous people in history, St. Paul has been honored in a special way:

> . . . But the big courage is the cold-blooded kind, the kind that never lets go even when you're feeling empty inside, and your blood's thin, and there's no kind of fun or profit to be had, and the trouble's not over in an hour or two but lasts for months and years. One of the

men here was speaking about that kind, and he called it "Fortitude."
I reckon fortitude's the biggest thing a man can have—just to go on
enduring when there's no guts or heart left in you. Billy had it when
he trekked solitary from Garungoze to the Limpogo with fever and a
broken arm just to show the Portugooses that he wouldn't be
downed by them. But the head man at the job was the Apostle
Paul. . . .[13]

Courage helps us to deal with two tendencies that permeate human
existence: the tendency to fear the unknown and the drive to flee
spontaneously from any object of danger. "Fright and flight"[14] can
block us from experiencing reality to its fullest. Courage enables us to
stand firm and fight when the situation calls for this type of response;
courage enables us to die to ourselves for the sake of life. Delegates,
knowing well what happens to most prophets in history, will have to
face many dangers and crosses. At times their courage will manifest
itself in patient endurance (the most difficult type of courage), while
at other times they will be called upon to pounce on evil.[15] Whatever
is not compatible with the gospel must be courageously questioned;
whatever is antihuman or subhuman must be diligently removed. Living courage is a great boon to the entire community, not just to the individual exercising that gift.

A third trait of the prophetic person, exemplified so clearly in the
life of Jesus, is that of *vision*. Delegates are called upon to have a
perspective of what religious life is, to be able to situate in their context contemporary issues, to sense the interrelationship among such
things as prayer, asceticism and the apostolate. The blind cannot lead;
only a person with vision can point the way. A guide who has not
been to a given territory, or loses the map which would lead there, is
no longer an asset to the group. Delegates without vision contribute
little in the attempt to provide meaning and direction for their communities. Two dangers have always plagued a healthy perspective:
myopia and ignorance. The first danger allows one to see, but only to
the end of one's nose—not a terribly helpful overview. Ignorance, the
second danger, can only result in a valley experience even though the
voice of the ignorant leader be forceful and filled with an apparent
self-confidence.

A number of responsibilities become obligatory for the prophetic
delegate. (1) A chapter delegate must be *informed*. Study and research
will be as necesary and as natural as breathing for such a person.
There is no excuse for not being aware of contemporary issues, the

movements of our present culture, the meaning and influence of history. The presence or absence of information is relatively easy to detect. (2) If a person is to be attuned to the mind and heart of God, *prayer* is necessary. Special emphasis should be placed on scriptural prayer since it is God's word which illuminates our understanding of contemporary issues. If the porters at the chapter doors should bar the uninformed, they should be twice as diligent in barring a person who does not pray faithfully. (3) A chapter delegate should be a person of *decision*. Newman in his *Apologia Pro Vita Sua* states: "Certitude is a reflex action; it is to know that one knows."[16] Study and prayer should lead us to this type of certitude which in turn enables us to make serious decisions, even though there will always be some element of risk if not doubt. Another facet in this process of decision-making is the willingness to assume responsibility for the decisions made. Indecisive and irresponsible persons should not be elected to chapters. The duties of being informed, prayerful and decisive are not acquired in a day—not even a week. Yet the delegate should be growing in each of these areas if the community is to be served well.

Delegate: A Wounded Healer

Jesus promised that when he had returned to the Father he would send their Spirit. That promise has been realized in all who have come to believe in the Lord. This Spirit is leading all back to the Father through Christ; this Spirit is a Spirit of love, joy and peace. Through the Holy Spirit, healing and reconciliation happen in our world today. A great vision of unity found in Pauline theology becomes a reality to the extent that people are living the life of the Spirit. Yet this vision of unity is premised on the tragic fact and acute awareness that fragmentation permeates creation. We humans are divided within ourselves and separated from our fellow humans, from God, and from the world. We are a wounded people, scarred and battered by our own sins and the sins of others. "Everything God has made has a crack in it."[17] Our vocation is to make all one in Christ, to reconcile all creation to the Father. The gift of the Spirit dwelling in the Church and in our personal lives enables us to begin this glorious and painful task.

The delegate as wounded healer is distinguishable by a sense of deep *compassion*. Graced with the ability to perceive things from the inside, the compassionate person has a knowledge of the heart and not just of external activity. The secret of the fox[18] is undoubtedly correct: "And now here is my secret, a very simple secret. It is only with the heart that one can see rightly; what is essential is invisible to the eye." Compassion promotes our seeing what is truly significant; it goes far beyond the inhuman limitations of our sensate culture. So often in Scripture, reference is made to the necessity of a new heart.[19] God's word urges us to grow in compassion and empathy. Insensitivity to the hurts and pains of others, even though these may be self-imposed, prevents the building of community. Compassion heals! Hopefully, every delegate has had the experience of being healed through the heartfelt concern of others. Perhaps the task of the doctor applies to all of us: "sometimes to cure, often to alleviate, always to care."[20] Compassion is care incarnated.

The destructive force of nuclear warfare is so obvious that no one can deny its effects; less obvious but extremely powerful in the psychological realm is the prevalent killer called judgmentalism. A delegate must be a *non-judgmental* person. This does not mean that one ceases making judgments, judgments which at times are sharp and painful. God has blessed us with reason and insight and we must ferret out the truth and the falsity of our lives and the life of the community. We cannot renege on our responsibility to find the truth and to speak it boldly. Judgmentalism, on the other hand, uses the faculty of reason but in an abusive way. Judgments are made, not on discernible consequences, but on motives which cannot be verified. Evidence is wanting, yet persons are judged and insinuations are made. This type of judgmentalism is characterized by intolerance (a demand that everyone live by my interpretation of religious life), a defensiveness and air of hostility, a lack of warmth and affability. A delegate, therefore, should have a delicate balance between tolerance of persons and intolerance of falsity; between respect for the individual and firmness in sticking to principles; between understanding the human condition and calling each other to growth. We come to realize that without the gift of the Spirit we cannot but fail in this stupendous task. Again we are helped in this area by realizing that we have been blessed in our personal histories with people who have refused to judge and condemn us, who have manifested an infinite patience in allowing us to grow through the stages of personal development. If we have been the object of judgmentalism, our experience should forever prevent us from venturing down that road of psychological and spiritual destructiveness.

The word of God provides light for our pilgrimage. In the prophet Micah, we are challenged by the Father's word:

> this is what Yahweh asks of you:
> only this, to act justly,
> to love tenderly
> and to walk humbly with your God (6:8).

The call to justice, charity and faith is clear. Interestingly, spiritual love has the quality of *tenderness*, a term which forcefully describes the manner in which we are to reach out to others in concern. It is possible to serve unwillingly, to meet needs because of duty, to heal out of necessity. This is neither sufficient nor healthy in an ultimate sense. God calls us to enter fully and generously into the lives of others. A tender love, a gentle concern, a warm respect characterize total love. Underlying this kind of love is the keen realization that human beings are terribly fragile. Indeed, "avalanches gather force and crash, unheard, in men as in the mountains." People with whom we live can be breaking apart inside without our awareness; a tender word and radical love can heal so many lives that are on the edge of despair. A chapter delegate would benefit from reading Fr. Kevin O'Shea, especially his article "Enigma and Tenderness" (see note 14).

The chapter delegate, a wounded healer, is challenged to fulfill certain responsibilities in this area. (1) The delegate must *face the negative* in self, others and the world. A recent cartoon showed a street cleaner lifting up the edge of a sidewalk under which he swept the city's debris. No healing can take place unless we honestly and courageously face that which is destructive within life. Exploitation and manipulation are too common to be ignored; these must be searched out and dealt with in a reasonable way. (2) The delegate should *face the positive* in self, community and the world. Just as dangerous as the rug syndrome is the denial of our unwillingness to recognize the vast potential waiting to be actualized in creation. Leadership qualities lie fallow because of fear; intellectual skills remain untapped because of a lack of challenge; talents stay on shelves for want of affective nutrients. "Our intellectual and active powers increase with our affection."[21] The truly great person has the vision to recognize the gifts of others. The delegate must perceive and promote the gifts and talents given by the Lord. (3) The delegate should *rejoice in life*. Nothing heals so quickly as genuine humor and authentic play. Joy is one of the signs of the Spirit's presence. It flows from an awareness of God's personal love and the gift of his life.

It is eminently unfair to demand of a single individual the multiple qualifications listed here. No one person could qualify in every area.

Consolation comes from the fact that religious chapters are not made up of only one individual. Rather, they are community affairs and the principle of complementarity comes into play. What one lacks, others have. The above job description is not so much one for individuals as it is for a community. Because of the blessing of pluralism, many communities could easily qualify. Tragic is the election in a community that allows a strong predominance of a single personality type. Once again, it is diversity that leads to life—a diversity grounded in concern for the kingdom.

1. The image of wounded healer is taken from Henri J. M. Nouwen's book by the same title.

2. Leo Tolstoy, *War and Peace*, trans. Louise and Aylmer Maude (New York: Oxford University Press, 1942) 1241. Used with permission.

3. C. S. Lewis, *Perelandra* (New York: Macmillan Publishing Co., Inc., 1944) 140.

4. C. S. Lewis, *Surprised by Joy: The Shape of My Early Life* (New York: Harcourt, Brace & World, Inc., 1955) 184.

5. Martin Buber, "Hope for This Hour," *Pointing the Way*, ed. and trans. Maurice S. Friedman (New York: Schocken Books, Inc., 1974) 222.

6. *Ibid.*

7. Meriol Trevor, *Newman: Light in Winter* (New York, 1963) 86.

8. Source unknown.

9. *Spiritual Renewal of the American Priesthood*, ed. Gerard Broccolo and Ernest E. Larkin, O. Carm. (Washington: United States Catholic Conference, 1973).

10. Gerard Manley Hopkins, "God's Grandeur."

11. The allusion is to Elizabeth Barrett Browning, "Aurora Leigh."

Earth's crammed with heaven
And every common bush afire with God;
And only he who sees takes off his shoes—
The rest sit around it and pluck blackberries.

12. Ralph Waldo Emerson, "The Over-Soul."

13. John Buchan, *Mr. Standfast*, quoted in C. H. Dodd, *The Meaning of Paul for Today* (New York: New American Library, 1920) 7.

14. Kevin O'Shea, "Enigma and Tenderness," *Spiritual Life* (Spring 1975).

15. See Josef Pieper's Thomistic treatment of fortitude in *The Four Cardinal Virtues* (Notre Dame, Ind.: University of Notre Dame Press, 1966) 117–41.

16. Earlier he writes, "In the first chapter of this narrative I spoke of certitude as the consequence, divinely intended and enjoined upon us, of the accumulative force of certain given reasons which, taken one by one, were only probabilities."

17. Ralph Waldo Emerson, "Compensation."

18. Antoine de Saint Exupéry, *The Little Prince*, trans. Katherine Woods (New York: Harcourt Brace Jovanovich, 1943).

19. See, for example, Jer 31:31-34; Ezek 36:24-28.

20. Paul Ramsey, quoted in *America* (May 1, 1976) 377.

21. Ralph Waldo Emerson, "Friendship."

15

Presence and Possibility
Beyond Death and Dying

In her book *On Death and Dying,* Dr. Elizabeth Kübler-Ross provided a tremendous service for countless individuals, families and medico-pastoral personnel by her dealing with the reality of death and the stages that lead up to it. Her descriptive, insightful categories of the various stages of dying (denial and isolation, anger, bargaining, depression, acceptance) explicate the process that many dying people journey through, indeed that the majority of people face in the death experience.[1]

It is with some reluctance that I make the following reflections lest they be interpreted as either a challenge to Dr. Kübler-Ross' findings or appear as unwarranted additions that cannot be verified. Yet, given the complexity of death and its inherent mystery, we are faced with the possibility that perhaps the five stages of death described above do not provide the human spirit with sufficient meaning to deal with the sense of futility and meaninglessness confronting the dying person.

In researching the stages of dying (denial through acceptance) the descriptive account is accurate since this is what most people reveal in their responses to terminal illnesses. As Edgar comments at the end of Shakespeare's *King Lear,* "Speak what we feel, not what we ought to say," so, too, the dying person tells it as it is: "I'm not going to die—I'm angry that life is being taken from me—just two more months, please—I'm depressed in this hopeless situation—I accept this moment as part of life." Each person approaches death from a specific, personal point of view, and his or her verbal and symbolic responses flow from this implicit philosophy.

We should note carefully, at this point, the historical elements that have shaped the contemporary mind in matters of life and death: rationalism, scientism, the Enlightenment, existentialism and many other movements. These philosophies contain an implicit concept of death: death is the end of the ball game; death terminates personal existence; death is the supreme evil; death is meaningless and thus life is ultimately absurd. The mass media, our educational institutions and various other cultural channels have molded the minds and hearts of people in an evolutionary way. The contemporary person, acclimatized by these forces and philosophies, approaches the reality of death by denying its approach, by venting anger at such a hostile foe, by bargaining for life at any cost, by despairing before this fearful and dark monster, by accepting the inevitable since it would only be worse to do otherwise. Sociological research simply delineates how the modern person lives out the values and attitudes handed down in history.

But what if death is not what it is thought to be? What if twentieth-century man and woman have been led astray by concepts, psychologies and cosmologies that are ultimately false? How does this affect the mystery of personal death? Could it be that death is not *the* evil; that death does not contain ultimate finality; that death is even a friend, the other side of existence containing a fuller life? What would the dying process and stages of death be like for a person who perceived death from the vantage point of a fuller life and as a type of birth? No doubt, given the moments of darkness and doubt, such a person would have to struggle with denial and anger, bargaining and depression. Yet a person with a faith-filled vision of death would move even beyond acceptance, the fifth stage in the dying process, to a sixth stage, *expectation*. In the very center of pain and suffering, there would be hints and glimpses of a richer and fuller life inspiring a person to long for this presence and joy.

Beyond Stage Five—Expectation

In an article entitled "Death: A Theological Reflection," Ladislaus Boros presents a perspective of death as a moment in which the dying person comes before God. Death is a birth, it is an encounter, it is a time of deciding for or against God's love. He states that "death offers us the first possibility of making a final decision, face to face with

Christ, in complete freedom and with the utmost clarity of mind."[2] This hypothesis is developed at some length but constantly returns to a new type of freedom gained through death:

> By experiencing death, therefore, man is liberated from everything that prevented him hitherto from seeing God face to face. Death therefore is liberation to true freedom. Through death man is delivered up completely to his God. He cannot any longer hide himself from God. His soul is—so to speak—transplanted into that infinite field where there is nothing but himself and his God. He stands now face to face with the risen Lord. Christ himself had to make his own the death-struggle, dying and death, so that every man who goes on the way of death might meet him suddenly in blinding clarity, so that every man—at least in death, would make a final decision, face to face with him.[3]

Objections to this "romanticism" can be heard; namely, otherworldliness, the great beyond of rest, spiritual panacea. These criticisms miss the point. To desire fulness of life in no way denigrates the beauties of the present moment; to long for complete truth and goodness does not discredit partial truth experienced now and the echoes of goodness shared among people; to yearn for total freedom does not prohibit the cosmic dance from beginning in one's personal life. Boros' insight is helpful here: "Man in death is also confronted with what he always surmises in all his knowing, that towards which he unconsciously strives in all his willing, what he embraces in reality in all his loving."[4] The above objections are fallacious; death is the most meaningful and affirmative act in human existence!

Death for Socrates

As reported by his faithful disciple Plato, Socrates, the great sage of Athens, was condemned to die, from all appearances not a terribly happy sentence. But strange to say, as the friends of Socrates gathered around their master to console him in this darkest of all possible hours, Socrates actually consoled them. The basis for this strange behavior lay in Socrates' vision of life and death, a vision not influenced by the forces shaping contemporary minds. From the available material on Socrates, there is no indication that he denied the reality of his own death; on the contrary, the literature tells us that his whole life was viewed as a preparation for death, a type of practice for this moment. Nor do the reports speak of anger or bargaining, though these cannot by that fact be absolutely excluded.

Their presence, however, would manifest a radical inconsistency with what has been handed down. Despair rested in his friends who misread the mystery of death since, for them, it meant only the loss of a friend and a teacher, and in this case, was the consequence of injustice. By contrast, we discern a haunting hope which dominates the spirit of Socrates. In facing his death, Socrates' attitude points not only to a radical acceptance but even more to a sense of expectation.

Was Socrates' approach to death based on an idealistic philosophy, the world of ideas? Certainly! But he was passing on in philosophic language a rich theological tradition that contained a vision of humanity and of the world far different from our own; a vision, I think, that is more accurate in its ultimate meaning than the vision of humanity and of the world offered during the past four centuries of crude scientism. Socrates believed in the gods, he was a man of faith and genius. This colored and gave meaning to his death and how he approached it.

The dominant tone in Socrates' view of death was that of longing. All during his long life he had searched for truth. He hungered for virtue and goodness in the ethical realm. Beauty and order were welcomed guests whenever they appeared. But Socrates realized well the incomplete nature of man's experience as well as the transitory element in all that is human. For Socrates the fleeting hints and shadows of truth, goodness and beauty perceived in daily life told of some transcendent Truth, Goodness and Beauty. He loved life too much to stop short of the fulness of reality. It was his conviction that through and beyond death he would participate fully in the object for which he searched. Thus death became a friend, a means of obtaining what he had always wanted. Hope filled his spirit as he drank the hemlock.

Death for Paul

Some four centuries after Socrates another pilgrim dealt rather directly with the reality of death. Paul, once a persecutor of the Christian community, experienced Christ in a profound way. In that encounter his life was turned around, his heart was deeply touched, and a new vision of life was received. No longer did he live his own life, but the Lord lived in him. No longer was life itself a supreme value because now Paul longed to suffer and die with Christ so as to share in his glory. Paul's vision of death and his very desire for it astounds the contemporary person:

Life to me, of course, is Christ, but then death would bring me something more; but then again, if living in this body means doing work which is having good results—I do not know what I should choose. I am caught in this dilemma: I want to be gone and be with Christ, which would be very much the better, but for me to stay alive in this body is a more urgent need for your sake (Phil 1:21-24).

All I want is to know Christ and the power of his resurrection and to share his sufferings by reproducing the pattern of his death (Phil 3:10).

For I am certain of this: neither death nor life, no angel, no prince, nothing that exists, nothing still to come, not any power, or height or depth, nor any created thing, can ever come between us and the love of God made visible in Christ Jesus our Lord (Rom 8:38-39).

Paul's vision of death implies a leaving of one world for another, the temporary for the eternal where Christ the risen Lord dwells in glory. This perspective of death leaves little room for denial, anger, bargaining or despair, though death, insofar as it prevents the meeting of urgent needs, does connote a negative element. What Paul's vision of death was before he experienced the love of Christ we do not know, but it was that love which altered the very essence of his life. If there had been a fear of death, the shadow that clouds human existence, it was now gone; if there had been old anxieties, they had now dissipated. As Saul no longer existed but only Paul, so now death had lost its sting and had given way to expectation of fulness of life.

A crucial problem in Paul's experience revolved around the question of freedom. The ability to accept or approach death with expectation and longing is premised on the development of freedom to the point where each of us has acquired radical decision-making responsibilities. Paul was caught in a dilemma, and we know that having the mind and heart of Christ grounded his freedom in the Father's will. Undeveloped freedom is synonymous with enslavement. Hence the immature person can only react, not respond to death. Developed freedom, on the other hand, implies a freedom from things, sometimes called detachment, by which there is no desperate clinging to material, psychological or even spiritual gifts.

Years of discipline and cooperation with grace are necessary before such an interior freedom and simplicity become a part of one's being. Paul appears to have reached a high level of detachment. Though he no doubt was close to relatives, friends and other treasured values, all of which could have controlled his life, he was able to relativize these in the light of a personal experience of Jesus.

Within the context of this religious experience and based on an acquired freedom, Paul could anticipate and even "want to be gone and be with Christ" and allow all the joys and goods that enriched his present life to become subordinate to the primary Good.

Paul's freedom "from" implies a freedom "for." The vacuum created by detachment is not necessarily healthy or desirous. To deprive ourselves or others of treasured relationships or possessions without a promise of something better would be unjust and cruel. Our powers and faculties have objects that bring fulfillment; deprivation as such can be highly destructive. What was the object of Paul's freedom "for"? Through his conversion experience, Paul gained a knowledge of who Christ really was. As God continued to grace Paul with zeal and the gifts of the Spirit, Paul lived ever more deeply the mystery of divine indwelling. Yet in the face of the realization that the Father's gifts and deeds were indeed precious, the apostle to the Gentiles centered his freedom on God himself—on the Giver more than the gift. Through the gracious redemption of Paul's freedom, death became an object of choice, for death now meant a means by which God would be encountered fully in Christ. Until freedom was thus transformed, death's face appeared as a sad and dark mystery.

Death for Jesus

The Christian is challenged to approach death in a manner similar to Christ's experience. Here we come to see that the life and passion of Christ are grounded in attitudes of acceptance and expectation. Mortification, self-denial, basic poverty is the air that Jesus breathes. The Christian life embraces these patterns which, if experienced in union with Christ, become rich moments of growth both in the human and spiritual dimensions.

Jesus knew of this approaching death; the signs became increasingly obvious that he would be destroyed. For the apostles this possibility would be incredible and untimely; by any human standard, brutal and cruel. Yet Jesus does not evidence hatred or even anger in the face of rejection, hostility and injustice. Undoubtedly he prefers to avoid pain. The deep anguish that can be felt by any sensitive heart who hears the words: "Father, if it is your will, take this cup from me," brings to the fore the humanity of Jesus. On the human level pain and death are repulsive and a cause of dread. On the human level the fear of the unknown, the violence done to the body, the uprooting of all that was loved and treasured are beyond description.

Jesus experienced all this and more, yet not at the cost of his central desire: to fulfill the Father's will. Because of his love of the Father, Jesus would endure all things whatever they might be. If need be, the betrayals and lies, the denials and injustices, the cruelty and apathy would all be endured. The Father's will, the reconciliation of all creation, was the perspective from which Jesus lived his life; a perspective which would provide significance to his saying "yes" to death, death on a cross. If death would promote the kingdom, if death would destroy sin, if death would prove to be the true and eternal passover, then Jesus would willingly and expectantly accept it because unity and peace lay on the other side. Here we stand awestruck at a great paradox: life coming through death.

Christ's passion was neither singular nor momentary. Preoccupied with the Father's ways and thoughts, Jesus' whole life was a type of dying process. In order that others might have life, he selflessly gave of himself. St. John's Gospel succinctly drives home the mission of Jesus: "I have come so that they may have life and have it to the full" (10:10). His time and energy were not his own. His obedience was a constant listening and responding to the movement of the Spirit. His consciousness of being sent into a "bent world" to heal broken hearts and to mend fragmented lives with compassion and love was keen and dynamic. Jesus died freely many times before his actual passion. Could it be that because he chose death early in life, he lived so fully? Thus when that fateful Friday came, his previous experiences had prepared him well to respond with a final "yes," so that the redemption of all creation would be realized.

Dying and death connote sadness and gloom, natural responses to such dark mysteries. Certainly Jesus had to deal with such feelings. Yet at a deeper level, in the depths of his heart, a painfully quiet joy existed in that Jesus focused on the good that would result from his total self-giving. Here there is a lack of self-consciousness common to all doers of good, an underlying joy and vitality in ministering to the needs of people, a charm and graciousness of someone respecting the uniqueness of others. The inevitability of death did not cause moral paralysis nor prevent a full participation in life. Jesus was not the victim of the pessimistic "why begin something if all ends in death." Love for life did not deter him from death, nor did impending death deter him from joyously serving others and sharing the life of the Father. Joy characterized the life of Jesus; joy led to great activity and total involvement.

Just as Jesus personally embraced all of human life, its joys as well as its sorrows, so he clearly expressed to all who would choose to follow him that they must accept and expect a similar death leading to life. The lesson was not easily learned then or now. When Peter attempted to deny the coming passion, Jesus strongly admonished him for his failure to live in the truth. James and John, angered at being denied entrance to a certain Samaritan town, would have had God destroy the city; Jesus rebuked them for their ignorance of what God was really like. When a mother sought honored positions for her sons in Jesus' kingdom, she was told that only those who drank from the cup could dwell in the courts of heaven. Peter, standing on the brink of despair after denying Jesus three times, felt the healing but painful gaze of forgiveness and understanding across the night air. The paschal mystery, the participation in the life-death-resurrection of Christ Jesus, permeates all of Christianity. To live in Jesus is to accept the whole package of sorrow and joy, death and life, the cross and the crown. Jesus summarizes these mysteries:

> Then to all he said: "If anyone wants to be a follower of mine, let him renounce himself and take up his cross every day and follow me. For anyone who wants to save his life will lose it; but anyone who loses his life for my sake, that man will save it" (Luke 9:23-24).

Death for C. S. Lewis

Socrates, Paul and Jesus, distant from us by more than nineteen centuries, might well appear to the sophisticated twentieth-century person as simply ancient, historical personages. One might wonder whether or not there are any moderns who would conceive of death primarily in terms of expectation and longing. C. S. Lewis, a recognized scholar of literature and a theologian of no small stature, has reflected on the mystery of death in several of his works. The following selections from his writings indicate to me that he viewed death from a perspective much in keeping with the hope-vision of Socrates, Paul and Jesus.

In his novel *Till We Have Faces*, Lewis seems to present his own personal experiences of death through the character of Psyche:

> "This," she cried, "I have always—at least, ever since I can remember —had a kind of longing for death." . . . It was when I was happiest that I longed the most. It was on happy days when we were up there on the hills, the three of us, with the wind and the sunshine . . . where you couldn't see Glome or the palace. Do you remember? The

colour and the smell, and looking across at the Grey Mountain in the distance? And because it was so beautiful, it set me longing, always longing. Somewhere else there must be more of it. Everything seemed to be saying, Psyche come. But I couldn't (not yet) come and I didn't know where I was to come to. It almost hurt me. I felt like a bird in a cage when the other birds of its kind are flying home.[5]

One is reminded of the common expression: "I was so happy I could have died." That apparently flippant statement contains a profound insight. When someone is really happy, being in the presence of a loved one or lost in play or rejoicing in another's success, there arises within the human spirit the desire that this ecstacy might last forever. The echo of truth and goodness and beauty in that moment cries out for continuance. Too quickly the human conditions of time and space terminate this touch of paradise. It passes and the wheel of life continues to turn. Lewis' reflection presents a type of desired existence in which there is a continuance of blissful moments.

Other quotations from his writings sketch Lewis' un-twentieth-century concept of death. Respectively, Lewis questions death as the prime evil, indicates that death necessarily precedes a new type of existence, and places death in the context of other realities of life:

They, of course, do tend to regard death as the prime evil, and survival as the greatest good.[6]

Nothing that has not died will be resurrected.[7]

And Digory could say nothing, for tears choked him and he gave up all hopes of saving his Mother's life; but at the same time he knew that the Lion knew what would have happened, and that there might be things more terrible than losing someone you love in death.[8]

Based on a philosophy not limited to time and space, Lewis' basic attitude toward death is optimistic and expectant.

Since C. S. Lewis belongs to the twentieth century, the influences of our times naturally affected his thought. When death struck home in a personal way at the death of his wife, whom he had married late in his life, Lewis wrote out his feelings in a notebook later to be published under the title *A Grief Observed*. Many of the entries could have been selected by Dr. Kübler-Ross as examples of the various stages through which people go who have experienced a deep loss.

In fiction, Lewis philosophized about death with much hope and expectation; in the midst of the reality, grief and sorrow rent his heart. What a difference there is to philosophize, to talk *about* something (death) and to be thrown into the reality of it. The first we control, the second controls us and catches us up into its mystery. However, as the final portion of his notebook shows, Lewis emerged from self-pity into the realization of joy that his wife had attained all that both she and he had hoped and longed for. In Lewis' experience we witness a person who, because of the cultural conditioning of our times, passes through all the stages from denial to acceptance, yet because of his faith perspective adds the sixth stage, expectation.

Death for Modern Christians

Our attitude toward death remains philosophical and abstract until the reality touches our lives in a personal way. The death of a parent or child, a brother or sister, a lover or friend shatters philosophies and abstractions even though they be formed with steel chains. The mettle of our belief is tested, and it is in facing the death of a loved one that we ultimately face our own death.

What our attitude will be is basically a metaphysical question, coming to rest on our concept of reality. Dr. Kübler-Ross' research delineates an implicit metaphysics lived by many people in their journey toward death. Necessarily, a philosophy and a theology of life are contained in our actions and attitudes. This chapter maintains that there is another metaphysics beyond the one commonly handed down to us today and often uncritically accepted. The alternative metaphysics, contained in the experiences of Socrates, Paul, Jesus and the writing of C. S. Lewis, posits ultimate meaning in the experience of pain, suffering and death. It further implies that since death gives entrance into a fuller, brighter world, it can and should be approached with expectation.

Death is inevitable. The manner by which we encounter it is not. This chapter has stressed that the death experience of Socrates, Paul, Jesus and C. S. Lewis was strongly colored with joyful expectation, traditionally called hope. Though we do not have much evidence that they passed through the stages of denial, anger, bargaining, and acceptance, this is not of ultimate importance. My thesis is that expectation-hope permeated this human experience and won out. Whether we call it stage six or conceive of it as the climate in which we are challenged to experience death makes little difference. What does make a difference is whether or not hope resides in our hearts.

Interestingly, the experience of death in the four cases described above were instances of persons who were not killjoys just biding their time in a dark, dingy world, but lovers of life in the here and now as well as givers of life to others. They died as they lived, filled with hope and trust in their saving God. A contemporary author describes well the Christian meaning of death:

> But, by His death and resurrection, Christ has transformed death from a blind alley into a passage to glory. At my death, I will be completely fragmented, torn apart, disintegrated. And, on the other side of death, Christ will put me together again, this time completely centered on Him.[9]

1. Elizabeth Kübler-Ross, *On Death and Dying* (New York: Macmillan Publishing Co., Inc., 1969).

2. Ladislaus Boros, "Death: A Theological Reflection," *The Mystery of Suffering and Death*, ed. Michael J. Taylor, S.J. (New York: Alba House, 1973).

3. *Ibid.* 143.

4. *Ibid.* 142.

5. C. S. Lewis, *Till We Have Faces* (Grand Rapids, Mich.: Wm. B. Eerdmans Publishing Co., 1956) 74.

6. C. S. Lewis, *The Screwtape Letters* (New York: Macmillan Publishing Co., Inc., 1961) 131.

7. C. S. Lewis, *The Weight of Glory* (Grand Rapids, Mich.: Wm. B. Eerdmans Publishing Co., 1949) 39.

8. C. S. Lewis, *The Magician's Nephew* (New York: Macmillan Publishing Co., Inc., 1955) 175.

9. Robert Faricy, S.J., *Spirituality for Religious Life* (New York: Paulist Press, 1975) 75.